BOW LAKE
Provincial Park

THE ALL-SEASONS GUIDE

Richard T. Wright

At 38 km (24 miles), Isaac Lake is the largest in the chain. It has changed little over the past century.

THE COVERS
Front: Kibbee Lake, embarkation point for the journey around the Bowron chain. Photo by John Mackenzie. **Back:** The top photo is of the north arm of Isaac Lake in the Cariboo Mountains. Photo by Ken Mather. The bottom one shows a grizzly enjoying a summer dip. Except during the salmon spawning period, the big bears prefer alpine country to the lowlands. Photo by John Mackenzie.

PHOTO CREDITS
B.C. Provincial Archives: 4-5, 9, 22-23, 30, 36, 60-61, 89 (top), 106 (top); B.C. Provincial Museum: 13 (top); Heritage House: 118, 119 (top); Mather, Ken: 101 (inset); National Film Board: 51 (top); Tourism B.C.: 13 (bottom); Wright, Richard T.: 45, 47, 51, 54, 69, 71, 75, 81, 89 (bottom), 98, 101, 106, 115, 119 (bottom).

Canadian Cataloguing in Publication Data

Wright, Richard, 1940-
   Bowron Lake canoe country

ISBN 1-895811-04-X

1. Bowron Lake Provincial Park (B.C.) — Guidebooks.
2. Canoes and canoeing — British Columbia — Bowron
Lake Provincial Park — Guidebooks. I. Title.
FC3815.B69W75 1994   917.11'75   C93-091726-X
F1089.B76W75 1994

First Edition - 1994

HERITAGE HOUSE PUBLISHING COMPANY LTD.
Unit #8, 17921 55 Ave., Surrey, B.C. V3S 6C4

Printed in Canada

The Author

This book by Richard Thomas Wright is an example of the author's talent for writing guide books and his love of the Cariboo and its rich history.

Well known as an outdoors and historical writer and photographer, Wright has traveled much of this province by canoe, cross-country skis and by foot, and has spent many summers and a few winters in the Cariboo.

He has had 20 books published, including *Canoe Routes: British Columbia,* and *Cross-country Ski Routes: British Columbia.* His most recent books are *In a Strange Land,* a pictorial history of the Chinese in Canada, and *Barkerville: A Gold Rush Experience.*

Wright worked as a journalist for several years, first with the *Quesnel Cariboo Observer,* and as managing editor of the *Cowichan News Leader* in Duncan, B.C.

He now lives in the Cowichan Valley on Vancouver Island where he and his wife, Cathryn Wellner, a storyteller and writer, operate Auchinachie Farm, specializing in heritage breeds and seeds. Wright continues to write, while he and Wellner frequently tour as storytellers.

They are currently working on a series of books on the Cariboo goldfields. The first is a collection of gold-rush folklore — the poems, songs, stories and superstitions of a turbulent era in the provinces' development. The second, *Whiskey Dealers and Fallen Angels,* will look at the other side of social life in gold-rush towns.

Dedication

In memory of Dan Culver, who always pushed the limits.

A view from a campsite on Lanezi Lake shows some of the permanent ice and glacial cirques that typify the Cariboo Mountains.

Prologue

There is always so much that is worth seeing in the wilderness;
but if that wilderness has witnessed the passage of men of one's
own race — raiders, traders or explorers — then something is
added to the scene and it comes alive through a human association, a past which we can share and understand.

R.M. Patterson, *Finlay's River*

Acknowledgements

Thanks go first to those who have travelled the lakes country with me: Susan Chernov and my oldest son, Richard, who have both seen the lakes in winter and in summer; Tim Cushman and Dave Lakeman whom I joined for a winter dog-team trip down Isaac Lake.

I was helped immeasurably by my wife, Cathryn Wellner, whose enthusiasm for the country and its stories was a constant support.

Ken Mather offered notes and suggestions after his trip around the lakes, as did other correspondents over the past few years. Herb Carter of the Parks Branch answered many phone calls requesting information.

Sandy Phillips of Bear River Mercantile opened her history files to me for more information on the people of the lakes, and the BC Archives and Records Service was again a source of many documents and records.

Jerry MacDonald, editor/publisher of the *Cariboo Observer*, the Cariboo's paper of record, helped immeasurably by offering free access to the paper's back issues. Many of the stories in this book were found in the paper's pages, often written by Louis Le Bourdais, who during the 1920s and 1930s faithfully tracked down Cariboo history.

The Cushmans, Frank and Tim, have always been a source of great stories. Since the original edition I have been able to ride Cariboo mountains and ski the circuit with Tim and hear yet more of Frank's stories.

When the original edition of this book needed support, friend Dan Culver stepped into the breech, as was his way. His friendship was a strength for many years. In July 1993 he fell into the cosmos while descending from the summit of K2. This book is dedicated to him.

The Parks people have always been helpful, including

Gerry Ferguson, who has been sharing stories and trails with me for over 10 years now, and Gord McAdams, late of Bowron and Barkerville; the rangers we met on the lakes and the trail crews who made our walking easier; and Gail Ross who found some long out-of-print material.

Appreciation goes to that late great cadre of 1970s naturalists, of which I was privileged to be a member, who added so much to the knowledge of the natural and human history of provincial parks.

The Barkerville archives were a great source for researching the Bowron story. Former curator Ken Mather opened the files to me and gave me space to work. Ron Candy later assumed that role, and together he and I prowled graveyards and backroads. Based on the erroneous assumption that he was a good navigator and that I had a rough idea where we were going, we managed to get lost in some great areas, and return. In addition, curator Bill Quackenbush was very helpful with this current edition.

In Victoria, the reference room folks at the B.C. Archives and Records Service were also a great help in the continuing search for history.

The people of Wells and Bowron Lake are special and many of them helped with this book without even being aware. Judy Campbell loaned me her Tomato house during the research period; Jennifer Morford, who periodically lives on the lakes, gave me leads and stories.

If there is one person who still epitomises the guides who once hunted and outfitted this area, it is Frank Cushman. I have met Frank on several trails and heard some good stories from him, and later had the opportunity to ride a couple of alpine horse trails with him. He is always a delight to be with.

Any outdoor expedition needs good equipment and in this regard I was helped by Ken Green of Carleton Outdoor Recreation; Allan Slade Agencies, who provided skis and cozy polypropylene for the winter trip; and Randy Hooper of Coast Mountain Sports. The late Dan Culver of Whitewater Adventures, David John Smith and Rochelle Wright loaned canoes and equipment at various times.

Author's Introduction

Bowron Lake Provincial Park, this geological oddity, this liquid parallelogram, is, we are told in the park brochure, a "magnificent wilderness of more than 121,600 hectares" (300,352 acres.)

After spending summers in the area and skiing the lakes in spring and winter, I had trouble with this description. Magnificent? Yes, but a wilderness is surely not boardwalks, shelters with stoves, direction signs, designated controlled camping, picnic tables and permits. As a consequence, this wilderness billing at first gave me a negative outlook. What changed my view was finding the quote of R. M. Patterson in *Finlay's River* that begins this book. He gave me a new perception of the park, one more indicative of the area. It was a perception that has become even clearer as I learn more of the Bowron Lake people.

Bowron Lake Provincial Park is not untouched wilderness, as will be evident in reading this book. It is a place where men and women who enjoyed nature have met with her (or him) on their own terms and thus affected the landscape. It is this association of people and landscape that Bowron offers, not "wilderness." Canadians have always found this connection to be strong; it has become part of our psyche, a measurable influence on our literature and art. And the canoe has become as much a symbol of Canadian travel as the Conestoga wagon was to the great migrations of the United States. Author Pierre Berton has observed that a Canadian is somebody who knows how to make love in a canoe. Here in Bowron Lake country canoe and landscape come together.

The history of the Bowron Lake region is closely tied to mining, trapping, big game hunting and resort style living, in that order. Where trappers, homesteaders and holidayers once tried to push back the wilderness, we canoe, hike, snowshoe or ski in a way unchanged for a century. In many places, visitors will be able to sense the ghosts of days past.

Among over 50 designated campsites on the Bowron chain is the one above at Lynx Creek on Isaac Lake.

A problem with identifying with these "ghosts of days past" is that some years ago Parks Branch officials decided that the Bowron Lake area should be returned to wilderness. This policy meant burning down old structures, tearing up the rail portages that Kibbee and others put in, and banning motors. Yet at the same time the increase in picnic tables, shelters, privies and aluminum ladder caches continued. One cannot find argument with any of the latter; they are simply the result of too many people.

The policy of "resurrected wilderness" is, however, a contradiction in terms. Paradoxically every old cabin, lodge or trail that is torched or obliterated robs us of a piece of the association we seek with our past and those who were here before us. And that is sad.

It was not until I really began to dig into researching this book that I realized just how little has been recorded about Bowron Lake. There are stories about Kibbee and his grizzly fight and a spate of articles on the Wendles and the Cochran's and, more recently, the Cushmans, but little else. In this book I have gathered some of that information, some of the stories of the lakes and the recorded information that will, I hope, help not only to bring back a flavor of the past but also enjoyment of the present.

Contents

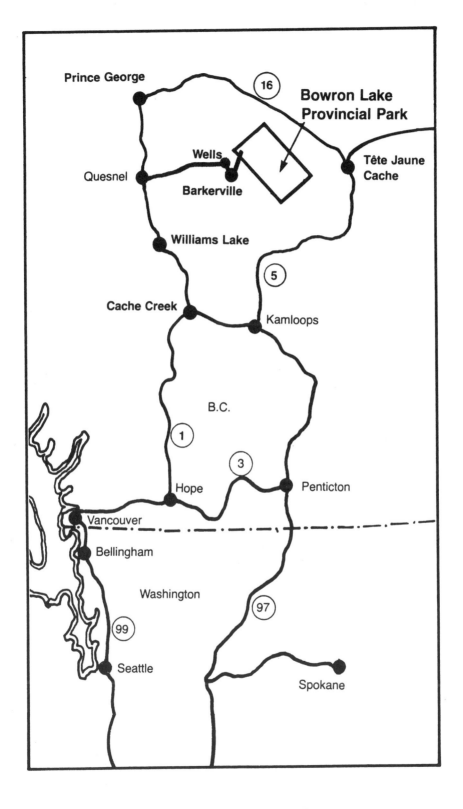

Chapter One
Introduction to Bowron Lake Provincial Park

The transition of the Bear River country from a wilderness into Bowron Lake Provincial Park was slow; a process that took over a hundred years of written history.

When Alexander Mackenzie made his way across the continent by land in 1792, 12 years before Lewis and Clarke crossed the continental United States, he met natives who called themselves the Takulli, the "people who go upon water." From them he heard of the Grease Trail that led him to the Pacific Ocean.

The fur traders who followed Mackenzie and Simon Fraser, who in 1808 was the first European to descend the Fraser River to its source, called the tribes of the Fraser and Nechako Rivers the Atnah, or Carriers. They were part of the Dene race, a word that to them meant "man," and were later classified as belonging to the Athapaskan language group which includes the South-west desert tribes of the Navaho and Apache.

Although the Dene society was one of matrilineal succession, the women were not the leaders. Brides were bought from the parents by various gifts. Divorce was possible, but women retained custody of the children, and were always assured of support for if her husband died, his brother took responsibility.

War was not a way of life, though they were not above the occasional battle with the southern Chilcotins or Shuswaps over hunting rights.

Death was what gave the Takulli their more common name of Carriers. Upon the death of a man, his body was placed on a pyre and his widow stayed with him until forced away by the flames. The bones were later gathered and placed in a bark container which the widow carried on her back for one year, except while sleeping.

Food sources for the Takulli included various native plants used not only for sustenance but also for medicines. Spruce tea, for instance, was a good cure for scurvy and used by miners as well as the natives. Alder bark was a laxative and cuts were covered with aspen roots. Mammals were killed by bow and arrows, snares and deadfalls. Smaller animals and waterfowl were trapped with submerged snares. As their name says, however, the Takulli were people of the water.

They were fishermen and, like spawning salmon, followed

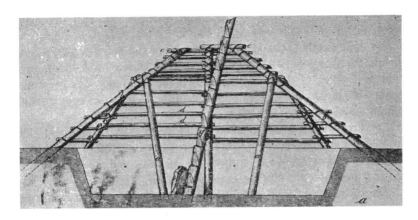

The framework of a keekwillee, or kekuli, that the Indians lived in during the winter. Access was by the notched center pole.

Salmon was a major food for the Indians. To reach their Bowron spawning ground the fish swam some 1,100 km (700 miles) up the Fraser and Bowron Rivers, fighting their way through scores of rapids.

the waters of the Bear (Bowron) River upstream to the chain of lakes. They fished by building weirs and barriers which funneled fish into removable baskets, and by suspending similar one-way baskets into streams. With natural fibers they fashioned dip nets similar to those still used today by natives on traditional, hereditary fishing rocks. In shallow streams they used fishing spears, often three-pronged, some with detachable heads.

During the spring and summer the people lived in permanent or semi-permanent villages of rectangular lodges. In fall and winter when they followed the salmon to lakes such as Bear they built dwellings called "Keekwillees," semi-subterranean circular pits covered with a conical structure of poles. They were usually built near a good food source.

One such village was at the outlet of Bowron Lake, near what is now the main park campsite. It was a village of about ten houses. (Unfortunately, it recently sloughed into the lake as a result of undermining and/or the Anchorage earthquake of 1964. Because the site was totally destroyed, any hope of archeological work is washed away.)

Evidence of these natives is scarce but there are a few clues. In 1828, Hudson's Bay Company Governor George Simpson made a journey from Hudson Bay to the Pacific Ocean. Chief Factor Archibald McDonald kept a journal of the trip and Simpson wrote a report on his return. In the vicinity of the Quesnel River he refers to the Naskotin band who "...generally hunt upon the range of mountains to the northeast (where Quesnel River takes its rise) and Bear Lake, where, from reports Beaver was formerly numerous — but subsequently nearly destroyed by the Iroquois." (The Iroquois were trappers the HBC brought from the Montreal area when the local natives of the Rocky Mountains were not aggressive enough in trapping furs.)

Simpson wrote that "...they obtain a few Beaver, some on the South banks of the Frasers River, and others go in a North Easterly direction toward a chain of lakes and Mountains bordering on Thompsons River."

This description no doubt refers to the natives of Bear, or Bowron, Lake. An 1867 map by HBC cartographer Alexander C. Anderson is less than perfect in its depiction of Bear Lake, but clearly shows a trail from the Fraser to the lake and a village at the outlet of Bear Lake. This village may not have been permanent. Perhaps it was used only for trapping beaver or fishing for salmon.

While the Carrier Takulli people knew of the attributes of the Bear River country, it seems that Hudson's Bay Company fur traders were only vaguely aware of this tributary of the Fraser

River. Likely, the Carriers were also responsible for trapping furs and taking them to the HBC post at Fort George at the confluence of the Fraser and Nechako Rivers.

Cartographers like Alexander C. Anderson took some time before they sorted out the rivers and lakes of the Bear Lake country. By 1867 Anderson was making accurate maps of the Cariboo Mountains gold country and the major streams, and while Bear Lake and River were located correctly, they were wholly inaccurate in size, shape, watershed and river route. Interestingly, he did indicate a major Indian trail from south of Fort George into Bear Lake and a village at the head of the river.

The demise of this small band of natives appears to be directly related to the Cariboo gold rush — the stampede in 1859 through 1862 that followed the discovery of gold on the Fraser River in 1858. Miners stayed and worked their claims but prospectors, the vanguard of miners, were not content to settle for the strikes on Quesnel River around Quesnelle Forks and Keithley Creek. They pushed upstream on a river we now call the Cariboo, through Cariboo Lake into what they called the Swamp River country. In doing so they appear to have discovered Sandy and Lanezi Lakes, and the west side of the chain — Babcock, Spectacle and Bear Lakes.

By the autumn of 1860, Gold Commissioner Philip Nind was reporting that George Weaver had been "prospecting on Bear River." That same summer George Harvey had explored the Upper Swamp River. In the spring of 1861, Nind submitted a map to Governor James Douglas showing the west side of the chain and Antler Creek, which he called the Bear River, flowing into the outlet of the lakes. The map was remarkably accurate.

When Antler and Williams Creek proved gold bearing, miners moved down the north slope of the Cariboo Mountains to the Bear River and down Williams Creek to Willow River.

In doing so, the Antler prospectors would have stumbled on Bear Lake, for Antler Creek flows into the outflow just a few hundred yards downstream of the lake. If they then chose to follow the larger stream they called Bear River (Bowron River), they would have eventually reached the Fraser River. It is unlikely any prospector could have passed up the opportunity for this exploration.

At the same time, prospectors were making their way upstream on the Fraser. By 1860 men like Timoleon Love, Tom Clover and party had pushed up the Fraser and over the Yellowhead Pass to Fort Edmonton, prospecting all the way. But they did not mention the Bear River by name. In January of 1861, however, Dr. J.B. Fiat, "...a French physician of considerable note...," now a packer at Fort Alexandria, had sponsored a fur-trading expedition above Fort George which resulted in a gold strike "on Bear River."

The strike was certainly small. There was no rush, but again in the following year Gold Commissioner Thomas Elwyn reported to Victoria that "...three miners report rich diggings on Bear River." But while the strikes were small in terms of the effect on the goldfields, they were disastrous for Bear River natives.

As miners moved into the area there were a few reports of Indians. Bishop Hills came through Williams Creek and Barkerville in 1862 and observed that "...there appears to be a village of Indians on Bear River some 60 miles from this. Six or seven of them wintered at Williams Creek." But for the most part natives were not mentioned.

It appears that by this time they no longer fished the lakes nor canoed the river. Robert Stevenson, a collector of stories who was on the creeks in the 1860s, wrote that smallpox raged through the Cariboo during the winter of 1862. "The small tribe of Bear Lake Indians of about 70 had all died but seven," he wrote. The smallpox epidemic swept from the coast through the interior of the province, wiping out thousands of natives. Many bands never recovered. Hazel Kibbee, Frank Kibbee's daughter, said the natives that contracted smallpox were taken to an island to die or get well, without aid. Most died, she said, and the island became known as Deadman's. The smallpox scourge of the 1860s was not the first, but likely resulted in the death of over a third of the native population.

The story got started, says Stevenson, that these Bear Lake natives had killed the ill-fated Rose and Johnson prospecting party. John Rose and William Johnson left Williams Creek in July of 1862 for a prospecting trip on the Bear River. They loaded their raft with five weeks grub and pushed off. That was the last they were seen. By October, newspapers were reporting them missing and Sebastapol, an old miner, was offering a reward for information. No information came out of the Bear River country.

Late the next summer three miners — Shibley, Cahill and Chapman — left Williams Creek on a prospecting trip. They went to Antler Creek and constructed a raft. Well down the river they saw two white flags of distress on each side of the river. At the first they found nothing. At the second they discovered "a dead body closely enveloped in a blanket. Near the head was a tin cup on which was scratched, 'Donald Monroe, of Inverness, Scotland, died June 1863, from starvation.' Another report says the words were "lost in the woods, born June 1825."

At Fort George an Indian told them that the Bear River tribe had murdered Rose and Johnson, and later buried them. They also reported that they had seen the bodies of over 100 Indians lying in and near the huts and that only three members of the tribe were alive. "Smallpox has left fearful traces of its ravages in their camp," they noted. "The campfires of the red men were extinguished forever. Their doom on this vast continent is surely sealed and their hunting grounds are passing into other hands." The story told to Neil Wilson, a trapper known as the "Swamp Angel," was similar. When he first arrived at Bear Lake and Swamp River, "Swampy" met an Indian woman who said she was the last of her tribe. The rest were buried on Deadman's Island, killed by smallpox. The sickness was punishment, she said, for the Indians killing some miners who prospected down the Bear River.

Prospectors had discovered much about the Bear River and Swamp River country by the end of the 1860s, but credit for most of the exploration likely goes to Fred Black who had a store at Keithley Creek in 1861. In fact, for a while the town was called Black's Store. But exploration was his main interest, and cartography his major skill. By January 1862, he had sketched an accurate map of the south slope of the gold-bearing Cariboo Mountains. He also knew the general direction of Antler Creek and Swamp River. He obviously kept up his exploration and gained a reputation for in October 1869 the citizens of Barkerville sponsored an exploration toward Tete Jaune Cache on the west slope of the Rocky Mountains. They hoped to forge a link in the east-west transportation chain.

Fred Black hired Charlie Fenton and they crossed from Antler Creek, near Barkerville, over to the head of Spectacle Lakes, which Black named Sand Lake. They cut along Babcock Lake into Swan Lake (now Sandy Lake) which he likely named for the swans that winter here. They passed along the south shore of Mountain Lake (Lanezi) and ascended the Swamp River to what they called Dominion Pass. They likely chose the name with a certain degree of enthusiasm and hope. Within a mile of the Swamp headwaters they hit a creek that flowed northeast "...which we named Castle River," and followed it to the Fraser River. The route would make an easy road, they reported.

Black's map is remarkably complete and accurate, indicating a vast knowledge of the country. It could easily be used today to canoe the circuit. Tributaries are mapped, including the Upper Bowron River and Pomeroy and Hucky Creeks. Harold Creek is correctly located and the headwaters of Betty Wendle. His map also shows that as early as 1869, Indian Point Creek was named. Black had clearly done a considerable amount of walking.

The next season, 1870, the Swamp Angel and Kenneth McLeod tried the same journey but only prospected into the

17

Swamp River. Another exploring party set out in 1871 when James A. Mahood led 23 men from Barkerville to Tete Jaune Cache, investigating a route for the Canadian Pacific Railway. They chose to go via Bear and Big (Isaac) Lakes, prompting the *Cariboo Sentinel* of August 18, 1871, to report: "Wilson, the fisherman of Bear Lake, commonly known as the 'Swamp Angel' goes, we believe, as guide. We are only sorry that Fred Black, who had been over the whole way to Fraser, is not here, as he could render much assistance; and according to his report, we think it would be better to follow the route across Antler to Swamp River, which he describes as level and practicable and only about 22 miles, sooner than make the unnecessary detour by Bear Lake."

Black was exploring new creeks in the Omineca country by now, and a few months later the CPR chose a route far to the south and the Dominion Pass route fell into disuse.

With confederation of Canada now a fact, the government, Gold Commissioner John Bowron in particular, was sending out small survey and exploration parties to try and find new routes and gold-bearing ground. Bowron was sure that lode gold, or quartz gold deposits, would be found in the mountains around Williams Creek. Every valley was probed and prodded.

The emergence of the Goat River as another route to the Fraser and Tete Jaune Cache was gradual. The river's mouth appears on Alexander Anderson's 1867 map, compiled from a number of sources, including his own 1832 and 1851 explorations. On his 1835 voyage down the Upper Fraser he notes the Atnah River and makes the notation, "...30 to 35 yards, swift, shallow, muddy. Septr/35." (Atnah was the fur-traders name for Indians of this region.) Then in 1871 the Honorable J.W. Trutch published a map of British Columbia which clearly shows the Goat labeled "R. aux Shuswaps."

It is hard to say who was the trapper, miner or explorer to first venture into the Goat River Valley, but certainly the Swamp Angel and Kenneth McLeod were precursors, and Black had mapped the Wolverine. They were also members of the party that named the Goat River during an 1886 expedition led by Robert Buchanan.

Their report to the Minister of Mines reads like a who's who of the Bowron country. It was addressed to John Bowron, "Gold Commissioner Cariboo," and was signed by Buchanan; George Isaac, miner, for whom Isaac Lake is named; Arthur Johnston, miner; Kenneth McLeod, trapper, whose name appears on McLeod Ridge on the Bowron Lake circuit and McLeod Creek which flows into the Goat; and his partner, Neil Wilson; the fisherman of Bear Lake, the Swamp Angel who moves through the lakes country history like a fall mist rising from warm water. They started from Barkerville July 15 and proceeded to Bear Lake (Bowron) and then continued to Wolverine Bay on Big Lake (Isaac). "Leaving the lake at this point," they later noted, "we followed up a stream to the summit or divide, between Big Lake and the Upper Fraser, having to cut our way through a heavy growth of brush and fallen timber so as to enable us to get our animals and packs along.

"After passing over the summit at a distance of about four miles we came to a stream, which we called 'Goat River'."

They followed the stream until day eleven when they built a cache. Then they continued, prospecting and finding some signs of gold. In summary, they felt the area deserved further investigation and recommended that a good trail be brushed out "so that miners could get through with pack animals."

The trail was used sporadically after that by miners, trappers and lumbermen wanting to outfit out of Barkerville rather than Quesnel or Fort George. Mileposts were erected and the trail cleared enough so that, at least in winter, a dog team could be mushed from the gold creeks to the Fraser's wide valley.

Packer Frank Aiken used the winter trail and left a good story. In January 1909 he was freighting supplies for Yellowhead Pass Lumber Co. timber cruisers who would arrive at the mouth of Dore River in the spring. He camped one night near the mouth of McLeod Creek and noticed the tracks of two men on snowshoes going up the McLeod's north side. "Strange," he thought. When he got back to Barkerville several days later the story began to unravel like a torn sweater.

In November 1908, with the temperature at the point where whiskey would freeze, a scarecrow of a man dressed in floursack patches, his red beard grizzled and hair unkempt, staggered into Barkerville from the Goat River Trail. He was carrying a sack of ore samples and dragging his partner, Bill Henderson. His name was Bill Spittle. "Well named," the postmaster later commented as he mopped saliva off the floor.

Spittle's story trickled out like grain from a broken feed sack. Originally an American, he had years ago sold out a homestead and quartz mine on Capilano River for a good price when the young city of Vancouver needed a waterline right-of-way. For a few years Spittle smuggled in Chinese aliens, but as the police made the coast hot for him he headed north. By 1900 he had been in the Williams Creek area long enough to run up a debt at Sam Rogers store. Now, eight years later, he was back.

Spittle and Henderson fell in with miners Charlie Baker and Jim McCurdie and convinced them to join in another winter trek to the Goat. They left Barkerville while Christmas decorations still hung in windows.

Once Frank Aiken heard this prologue he decided to check out the snowshoe tracks. On his next trip he tied his dogs at the McLeod and headed out on snowshoes, for obvious reasons known as "misery slippers." The trail ended on a jackpine bench. He found snowshoes, then a burned-out fire. Crouched nearby and fallen over the fire were the frozen bodies of Baker and McCurdie. The snowshoe tracks were explained, but the story's end would not be uncovered until the spring thaw.

Spittle had promised Baker and McCurdie winter provisions in return for partnership, but when they reached the Fraser River cache the supplies had been sent to Fort George. In danger of starving, Spittle went to the cabin of two Columbia River trappers, Steinhoff and Bogardus. They did not have sufficient supplies to winter the men but offered them enough to return to Barkerville. Baker and McCurdie accepted and headed back. Unfamiliar with the trail, they took the fatal turn up the McLeod. These were the tracks Aiken had found.

Spittle and Henderson stayed on the Fraser River. When Steinhoff and Bogardus were away they raided their cabin and headed for a Tete Jaune Indian camp. They stayed until spring — when the police came in. Henderson got four months. Spittle was taken down the Fraser by Frank Aiken, unable to walk on his frozen feet, plucking off toes as he went. After weeks in hospital at Lytton, he was given a ticket to Seattle and persuaded to use it.

When the Grand Trunk Pacific Railway was completed along the Fraser River from Eastern Canada to Prince Rupert in 1914, the Goat River Trail was less advantageous as a supply route and fell into disuse. Maps, however, still showed the dotted line and periodically someone tried to push through. In the 1950s George Gilbert, mineralogist and surveyor at the Wells Cariboo Gold Quartz mine, and Orphir Hamilton, assistant forest ranger at Penny, made a trip through. The trail had disappeared and the going was incredibly tough. They did find three old cabins and two mileposts but said they would never do it again.

Since the early 1900s, it has been a favorite election topic for politicians, and still resurfaces periodically as the answer to the Cariboo's transportation problems.

Whether the Goat River Trail still exists depends on the definition of a trail. In a 1992 study, Judy Campbell says "...in its current state it should technically be considered a 'route,' not a 'trail'." The old cut can still be seen near the McCabe's Lodge site on Indianpoint Lake and many maps still show a hesitant red line stretching from the Fraser River along the Goat and the lakes to Bowron Lake, indicating only the unreliability of maps. Wilson and McLeod seem to have been the first in the northern end, and for several decades they seem to have had a monopoly on the traplines. They sold to J. Wells Moxley, and he sold to Frank Kibbee in 1900. From then on the area began to see increased interest.

On a 1912 map a man named Develt had a cabin on Indianpoint Lake and Tom and Harry Brierley had two on Isaac. Up the Wolverine and Goat Rivers, Kenneth McLeod had a cabin, as did McGilliam. Beech LaSalle had two cabins on the route.

The end of World War I and programs to get returning soldiers onto the land resulted in a flurry of pre-emption surveys on the Bear River. During the 1920s there were over 15 families, or individuals, trapping or farming around Bear Lake and River, or Bowron, as it was now frequently called. They included Frank and Anna Kibbee, Joe and Betty Wendle, Floyd DeWitt Reed and his friend, Morris. Albert Littlefield, George and Mary Turner and Harold Mason and his wife. George Gilchrist and then the McCabes, the Brierley brothers and the Thompson brothers were east from Kibbee to Isaac Lake. Jim Kenny and L. Reid were trapping on Spectacle Lakes, and the Anderson brothers, Maurice and John, were trapping in the south end.

Down river were Henry Rivers, James Duffy, James and Lutie Cochran and William Bowron. The local papers were enthusiastic in reporting on what a good farming area it had become, with clearing and home building flourishing. At the same time, Kibbee and Wendle were bringing in hunting and fishing parties, men who would come back year after year to enjoy the country.

Major Harlan of Seattle was a regular visitor. Baron von Hirsch of Germany was a client of Kibbee, and Chester Ellsworth, a member of the California Long Beach Adventurers Club, came to Bear Lake frequently to add to his "...wonderful collection of ... trophies of his hunting trips to this province." He also looked around for property and brought up several friends.

Walter T. Hoover, a Los Angeles realtor, mining man and sportsman, came to hunt grizzly in 1920 and returned for several weeks each summer and fall for the next 15 years. He bought a 2-ha (5-acre) lot on the lake's south shore and built a fine summer home. Hoover realized that Fred Wells' mining finds would precipitate a rush, so he secured options on several miles of the Cariboo mining belt and brought in several companies to work them. In the winter of 1932-33, thousands of mineral claims were staked two and three times in snow four to 20 feet deep. Hoover loved B.C. and died at Qualicum Beach on Vancouver Island in June 1936.

Local editorials heaped praise on the area and urged the

Isaac Lake near Lynx Creek. The big-game guides of the 1930s and their clients were among those who started the movement that resulted in the Bowron chain evolving into today's provincial park.

completion and improvement of the Los Angeles to Barkerville Highway. To increase the salmon run, a million salmon eggs were placed in the Upper Bowron River for several years in a row.

It was becoming clear to a few that this was a special place. It was also evident that the area was being depleted of its wildlife. Louis Le Bourdais, later a Member of the Legislative Assembly, wrote that in the last "...twenty-five years hundreds of moose, scores of caribou and bear, have been killed. Scarcely a dozen marten are left where there were thousands in Swampy's time. Stalking game from the lakes was too easy for hunters, and the lakes made light work for winter trappers. Five years more and it would be too late."

Thomas McCabe, an enthusiastic naturalist, and Fisheries Inspector and ardent photographer John P. Babcock, who had been coming to the lakes for 18 years, began lobbying for the area to be protected. Joe Wendle backed the proposal, as did some high ranking provincial police officers. The Game Commission came to have a look. Babcock brought Chief Justice Gordon Hunter "for the mere joy of seeing the wild life."

In December 1922 Babcock wrote to the local paper to try and explain a conservation idea "...opposed by many well-known residents of Barkerville." He argued that protecting the inner lakes and allowing hunting on the outside of the lakes would

provide a sanctuary where animals could breed. He used Yellowstone and Glacier National Parks as examples.

Within months of Babcock's letter, the Game Commission approved a 240-square-mile reserve. The *Cariboo Observer* noted that "...the people of the Barkerville district were almost unanimously opposed to the refuge, and we presume they are still, as in their opinion no sanctuary is necessary in such a sparsely settled district."

Farming seems to have taken second place at this time. Tourism was now the attraction. In May 1927 the *Cariboo Observer* reported that "Joe Wendle is showing a certain amount of vision by erecting a large building, presumably a hotel.... Harold Mason is still working on his chateau across the lake; once finished it will lend elegance and charm." But the familiar Cariboo lament was still heard in the same report: "Just what the government's intentions are toward converting into a highway the present cross between a wagon road and a trail which leads from Barkerville to Bowron Lake, is a subject that should be of interest to every individual in the Cariboo."

There were even rumors that Western Canadian Airways was going to be making flights to the lake. On a sunny day in August 1929, 200 people came from Barkerville to witness the first landing. But the rumor proved to be false.

Frank Kibbee was appointed Game Warden for the new reserve, taking over from George Turner. Kibbee wanted people to enjoy the area and was instrumental in having narrow gauge railways built over some portages to ease the passage of boats.

Howard Harris in his book, *Ten Golden Years*, says that in the late 1930s the Forest Service had a youth camp at Spectacle Lakes portage. Ties were cut and two-by-fours freighted in for a new ferry system to replace Frank's old one. Mine car wheels were donated by Cariboo Gold Quartz Mining Co. The rails extended right into the lake, where boats were loaded and with a windlass hauled ahead. The railway was still being used into the 1960s.

Grover Youngs saw the potential for a lodge and built high above the lake at the north end. Now known as Becker's Lodge, it has remained a popular destination. In those days the trails were rough, and long. Because it was not common to take a boat all the way around, boats were placed on each lake and travellers hiked from boat to boat.

Responding to reports of the beauty and natural history of the area, the Parks Branch placed part of the area under reserve in 1948. It was extended in 1951 when staff began reconnoitering the area and drawing up proposed boundaries for a new provincial park. In 1961 the provincial government made a land trade. Hamber Provincial Park on the B.C. -Alberta border was reduced by three-quarters of its size, and 120,000-ha (296,400-acre) Bowron Lake Provincial Park was created from the old game reserve. Later purchases brought the park to its current 121,600 ha (300,352 acres).

By 1965 it was considered remarkable that 150 canoes per year were using the circuit. The park has now reached its capacity, and a limit of 50 per day has been set. In 1971 the park was increased in size when Arnold McKitrick sold land at the head of the lake to allow room for a campground.

The Bowron Lake Park established in June 1961 did not, however, have the "height-of-land" boundaries proponents had hoped for. Boundaries were moved just beyond the lakes, one result being that logging has been an increasing source of visual blight and auditory pollution. Logging on the west side of Spectacle Lakes has been visible for years, and a decade old massive clearcut at Wolverine Bay gives a less than pristine view. Hunter Lake has been overfished, the consequence of logging road access on the south. Betty Wendle Creek, unfortunately, is scheduled for logging, a scar that will be visible from Isaac Lake. In addition, the headwaters of the Cariboo River have major cutblocks mapped out.

A shortcoming is that the current boundaries do not reflect entire ecosystems. A B.C. park planner has said that "Bowron boundaries were not established on purely ecological criteria."

A proposal reflecting the concerns of various groups and individuals has resulted in the Cariboo Mountains Wilderness Coalition calling for the Wolverine watershed, though logged, to be added to the park, as well as the drainage of Betty Wendle Creek and the Cariboo River. The group also suggests a reserve connecting Wells Gray Park with Bowron.

The protection of the Bowron Lake area was first meant to provide a sanctuary for wildlife. When it became a park in 1961, it was with the idea of protecting an unspoiled wilderness and magnificent Cariboo mountain scenery. Recently, there has been recognition that the wilderness aspect has always been a misnomer of sorts, and one hard to maintain with current usage. It hasn't been a wilderness since the first trappers arrived over a century ago.

What is being preserved is a slice of life that no longer exists, the axe marks where men and women tried to settle and scrape a living from the land. These blazes and clearings, within a magnificent landscape cut from a wilderness, are what make Bowron Lake Provincial Park such a gem — a park unique to the interior of British Columbia.

The Bowron River, part of the unique Bowron circuit.

Chapter Two
People of the Lakes

John Bowron

John Bowron, for whom the park is named, arrived in the Cariboo in search of gold in 1862 as one of the Overlanders, a group of 250 men and one woman who crossed the vastness of what is today the prairie provinces from Upper and Lower Canada (today's Ontario and Quebec) by land rather than take the alternate route via the Isthmus of Panama. Their journey by Red River carts, on foot and, finally, on rafts took five months. While some of these men quickly returned to the East, approximately one-half stayed to mine along Williams Creek. Many became the leading pioneers of the province, with Bowron one of them.

John Bowron was born March 10, 1837, in the village of Huntingdon, Canada East (now Quebec). His father was a Yorkshireman who had emigrated to New York in the early 1800s and set up a business in lumber and general merchandise. During the War of 1812 he moved to Huntingdon to settle and married Sarah, daughter of Colonel Odell.

When news of the new British Columbia goldfields reached Huntingdon, John Bowron was 25 years old and studying law. The tall slim young man took only a moment to consider, then packed up and joined the Huntingdon Company of 25 to head west. This company of men was to become an integral part of Barkerville's life. They left the St. Lawrence in April and arrived on the Quesnel River in October.

Bowron wintered in Victoria and then in the early spring he and partner-cousin Bill Schuyler headed north to the gold creeks. John did whatever work came along for the first few years, including cleaning the blacksand which held the fine gold from mining operations and looking after the library. While he maintained an interest in some gold claims, he took on an increasing number of responsibilities. In 1864 he was librarian; 1866, postmaster; 1872, mining recorder and Richfield constable; 1875, government agent and, in 1883, gold commissioner.

While living in Barkerville, Bowron met Emily Penberthy Edwards, a young woman whose mother and stepfather ran a hotel at Richfield, the original Williams Creek town above Barkerville. In August 1869 she married John Bowron.

The Bowrons had five children: sons Archie (who died at seven months), Eddie and William; and two daughters, Alice and

Lottie. John and Emily were active members of the Cariboo Amateur Dramatic Society. Bowron survived several changes of government and as a courteous, kindly, generous man, won the respect of citizens in his government role.

John Bowron believed that the true wealth of Williams Creek would be found in the "mother lode," or veins of gold quartz. Although he was scoffed at, he persisted and eventually convinced the government to put some money behind quartz exploration. When his beliefs were proved accurate there was a flurry of excitement, but costs were too high and capital investment money was short. No attempt was made to retrieve the gold until the opening of the Cariboo Gold Quartz Mine in the 1930s.

Emily Bowron died in Barkerville in 1895 at age 45. Two years later John, then 60, married 33-year-old Elizabeth Watson at Victoria and they had one child. John Bowron died in Victoria on September 6, 1906, soon after he retired. Elizabeth died in 1922. Daughter Lottie married Dr. George Tunstall, but when he left for Kamloops she stayed in Barkerville. She later moved to Victoria but returned to Barkerville periodically for many years and was one of the pioneers who lobbied to have the town declared a historic site. She died in 1964. Reminders of the Bowron family include the lakes and the restored homes of John and Emily and William in Barkerville.

George Isaac, Ken McLeod and the "Swamp Angel"

While John Bowron was trekking west across the plains of what was then called Rupert's Land and rafting the Fraser River, another easterner, George Isaac, was travelling to the goldfields via the Panama route.

Isaac was born in Ireland in 1833, third son of William Isaac and Jane Nixon. In 1843 the family escaped the potato famine of Ireland as part of the greatest migration in history. They spent three years in Toronto. By 1846, at 13, George was working as a road builder, and for the next 16 years in lumber camps.

Isaac heard the stories of the 1858 Fraser River gold rush and decided he was going there. By 1862 he had earned enough money to pay his passage down the eastern seaboard, across the Isthmus of Panama and up the west coast to Victoria where he arrived on August 4, 1862.

He arrived in the Cariboo in 1864, an impressive man 6'4" tall, and weighing over 200 pounds. He was well described as "...an axe-handle wide across the shoulders and built as solidly as a stone out-house with the door shut."

For the first two years there is no record of Isaac but by 1866 he is back doing what he knew best — swinging an axe. He contracted with Conklin Gulch Sawmill to furnish 50,000 feet of logs at $25 per thousand. By 1869 he was operating the mill with a Mr. Baker.

Sometime in the next five years, Isaac put his axe aside for a shovel and gold pan and joined three other men — Hobart Flynn, Kenneth McLeod and Wilson, the Swamp Angel — to prospect the Willow and Bear River country. Isaac maintained a long partnership with Johnson, McLeod and Wilson for in 1886 they set off with several others to blaze a trail along the Goat River to the Fraser River. (See the Goat River stories.) Isaac was well identified with the Bowron country by this time for a 1887 map has replaced the name Big Lake with Isaac's Lake.

In 1895 Isaac, Johnson and two other men were running a tunnel through bedrock on Stewart's Creek, and reported to be bringing good pay, except for a lack of water. Isaac didn't place all his faith in one claim for at the same time he had claims on Antler Creek and Big Valley Creek.

By the early 1900s Isaac was still involved in mining but not in an active way. When he posed for a photo with other Barkerville old-timers in 1907 he was no longer the 6'4" youth who had arrived in the first days of the gold rush, but a bent old man, bewhiskered and walking with a cane.

On August 31, 1912, Isaac visited a friend and late in the afternoon came home to rest before dinner. When his Chinese cook went to call him he had "passed into the great beyond."

Less is known of Isaac's partners, Kenneth McLeod and Neil Wilson, the Swamp Angel. They were present with the earliest miners but supplemented their digging with fishing. Wilson was often referred to as "The Fisherman" and his nickname "Swamp Angel" comes from the Cariboo River country he frequented, at that time called the Swamp River. Swampy was a black-bearded Swede, at 6'6" bigger than Isaac.

Hazel Kibbee, daughter of pioneer Frank Kibbee, said Swampy was broad shouldered and able to pack 200 pounds. "I have never known anyone who pretended to be old enough to know where old Swampy came from. He was brought up among the Indians and was here when the Indians were dying of small pox." That puts Swampy on the lakes in 1862.

McLeod, his young partner, was as short as Swampy was tall. He was born in Scotland in 1840 and in 1859 emigrated to Canada to work as a Hudson's Bay Company clerk. When the Cariboo gold rush flamed in 1862 he was working at Fort George, (today's Prince George) and, like many other indentured servants of the HBC, deserted for the lure of gold.

The two formed a business partnership, catching and selling Bear Lake fish, charging 37 cents a pound or an ounce of gold for one sockeye salmon or a dozen rainbow trout. The partners had a fishing station on Bowron Lake, where McLeod later had a large house and acreage. He also had a cabin in Barkerville. As miners left Williams Lake and the market for salmon died, the two men turned to trapping. McLeod ran a trap line up Wolverine Creek toward the Goat River where a mountain and creek are named for him. Their cabins were the essence of economy — two logs on one side, four on the other, sloped roof, no windows, eight by ten feet. "It's plenty of room for a man and his dogs," McLeod would say.

Though partners, the two men were seldom at the same cabin. One winter, about 1890, McLeod had arranged to meet Swampy at their Bear Lake cabin. When he got there the fire was cold so he headed for the Indianpoint cabin. Swampy was there, helpless with a bad back. McLeod lashed him to a toboggan and, with much protesting from Swampy, headed for Barkerville, 20 miles away. McLeod left him there and headed back out. He never saw Swampy again for the old Swede died soon after. He willed McLeod all he had — two bear traps and a canoe.

Not long after, McLeod sold the traplines to J. Wells Moxley, while his house in Barkerville went to Frank McCarthy in 1910. Hotelman Andrew Kelly had told his son to make sure McLeod had a place to stay when he got old. But McLeod had been independent all his life and did not want charity. He left the Cariboo and checked himself into the Old Men's Home in Kamloops. He died a month later in February 1911.

Frank Kibbee

In the summer or autumn of 1900, a 33-year-old American rode into Barkerville from the Sweetgrass Hills in Montana. He was trail weary and crippled from two gun shot wounds — one self inflicted, one from a bar-room fight. His name was Frank Kibbee and when he heard J. Wells Moxley had his trapline in the Bowron Lake area for sale, he bought it.

When Frank Kibbee arrived he already had more stories than Barkerville had shovels, and legends grew around him. Not the least of these had him riding and being wounded with the U.S. Cavalry during Custer's raid on Sitting Bull at the Little Bighorn River in 1876. Although Frank was only ten at the time and there were no survivors, it was a fine story.

Kibbee's family had moved to Montana when the West was still being settled. His father died when he was 14. Two years later he was using his father's old 10-gauge shotgun and shot a charge through his coat, wrist and hand. When doctors wanted to cut off the arm he refused. "All they done was trim off'n a few slivers a bone that's stickin up like a bunch porky quills, plas-

John Bowron and
his two daughters,
Alice and Lottie,
about 1900.

Frank and Anne
Kibbee and their
daughters in 1925.

tered some adhesive tape back and front and drove off," Kibbee remembered.

"I used carbolic acid and a silk handkerchief, drawing the silk through it every day and sluicing 'er good with a powerful mixture. Them fingers cords was all chawed up and looked like pieces of black rope, so my brother and me took a pair of scissors and snipped em off at both ends. That's why these here fingers — first and second — ain't no good."

Kibbee splinted his hand with a board, but a year later a horse fell on it and broke it. "That's what put the hump in it."

Two years later Kibbee was trapping in North Dakota and went to a dance hall to relax. A fight started and he was shot in the leg. Again, doctors wanted to remove the leg. Again, Frank said no, and hightailed it for the trapping camp where with "arnicky powder and brandy they fixed it up."

His mother had a stroke after his father died and for 18 years was an invalid. Frank stayed in Montana on a place he had pre-empted until his mother died in April 1900. That was when he saddled up and headed for the Cariboo.

Kibbee developed Moxley's trap line and in 1907 on the east side of the Bowron River built the first home on the lake. This log cabin still stands near Bear River Mercantile. In 1915 he built a two-story log home near the present Government Wharf.

Frank Kibbee married twice. His first wife was Emma, a native woman, of whom we know little. A few years later Emma was gone and Kibbee decided it was time to marry again. Because women were scarce in the Cariboo he followed the time-honored tradition of advertising for a mail-order bride. He sent his letter to the nearest paper, the *Ashcroft Journal,* which had a rather small readership. Fortunately, his letter was so humorous and inventive that it became the subject of a *Vancouver Province* editorial.

Kibbee received 65 answers and narrowed the applicants to two on whom he was "...willing to pay the freight." His offer was accepted by an English woman. On May 23, 1912, the *Cariboo Observer* reported that "Frank Kibbee, the well-known trapper and guide of Bear Lake ... leaves on Friday's stage for the coast. It is rumored that he intends returning with a bride. Success to you Frank."

In Vancouver on June 4, he married Annie Ormond. On June 8 the *Observer* noted that Kibbee "...returned yesterday with his bride."

Annie was concerned about Frank's safety in an unforgiving backcountry and encouraged him to take a partner. So that fall he teamed with Frank Conners, described with typical Kibbee forthrightness as "...a greenhorn out of Barkerville at the end of prolonged spree." For Kibbee, his choice of a partner was nearly fatal.

In October 1912, Kibbee had set a bear trap a quarter mile or so from his house where a grizzly had been eating salmon he had dumped on his garden for fertilizer. When Kibbee and Connors went to check it, the trap, the log toggle and the bear were gone. However, a bear dragging a log leaves a distinct trail so they set off to track it down, Kibbee carrying his .44 Frontier Colt and Conners the 30-30 rifle. Periodically there was a devastated area where the toggle had hung up and the bear had destroyed the encumbrance. Conners was lagging behind, shooting spruce grouse, which made Kibbee angry. They were looking for a grizzly, not a bunch of feathers.

Finally they met the bear, crawling over a windfall, weary from dragging the trap and toggle. "Shoot now," Kibbee shouted, but Conners didn't fire. When they found the bear again it was on a hogback, 90 feet away and 60 feet higher, standing on its hind legs and roaring. With good reason, it was one angry bear.

Kibbee yelled for the rifle, drew his .44 and fired, hitting the bear in the neck. It then charged. Kibbee grabbed the rifle from Conners and waited for a clear shot. One shot would do it, he figured. At 12 feet the charging bear broke clear. Kibbee pulled the trigger. The only result was a click. Conners had emptied the rifle at grouse.

The bear then hit Kibbee. The trap and toggle smacked his chest and broke three ribs from his backbone. Conners headed for a tree. It was now bare hands against bear claws. Conners would later tell the newspaper that, hearing the noise, he rushed forward and shot the bear with a revolver, killing it instantly. Kibbee remembered it differently.

The grizzly planted its good foot on Kibbee's chest and started tearing at him with its teeth. It tore out a row of teeth and the right cheek, splitting his jaw bone. It then tried to get his head in its jaws. Frank kept pushing it off with his crippled arm. "I give it to him to chaw on so's he would let my haid alone. My face never was one a woman would look at once, let alone twice, but it was the only one I had and it suited me all right. I wanted to hang on to as much of it as I could."

The bear put a tooth into Kibbee's eye socket, trying to rip his skull, but somehow Frank pried it out and the teeth raked his scalp. The bear "...divided this old dome of mine off into town lots better'n most surveyors could a done," he later summarized.

The bear was tiring from loss of blood and it turned and limped off, allowing Kibbee to get at his pistol. But the enraged bear charged again, grabbing and chewing on his shoulder and arm. Kibbee tried to get Conners to come and help, but fortunately the bear then crawled into a thicket where it died. Despite his terrible injuries, Kibbee walked home. The next morning Dr. Callahan came and did a quick stitching job, feeling he was only making a corpse presentable. But six weeks later Kibbee came into Barkerville with J. D. Cochran to have some broken teeth extracted. Kibbee said he expected to start trapping on his return.

But this was not Kibbee's year. His first mistake was hiring Frank Conners, the second was not firing him. Weeks later the two headed out for Sandy Lake to get traplines in order. A few days later, Kibbee was crossing a beaver pond where the water had receded from under the ice and crashed through. The icy water was bad enough, but he had tied his revolver to his belt without a holster which Conners had left behind. The gun snagged and discharged into his leg, the bullet travelling from his hip to his knee.

That night Conners, who had been trapping on what they called Little Lake (now Skoi), arrived to find Kibbee in his bunk. His knee was badly swollen and discolored, and he was in severe pain. With help being a long way off, they decided to operate. Kibbee made his own first incision, then Conners dug down with a knife, located the .44 slug and hooked it out with a piece of wire. Kibbee knew the lakes were freezing and wanted to canoe out that night. Conners wouldn't go.

"Well, the long and the short of it was I was 23 days gettin' out, on a stretcher, afoot with a crutch, on a sled and finally in a canoe," Kibbee well remembered.

His recovery took a little longer this time, and his leg would thereafter "go kilkipy" (haywire) on him, but recover he did and was back at work before the next hunting season. Meanwhile, his "...cultus partner skinned out with the winter's catch." In today's language, Conners had ripped him off.

Although Anna had no idea what she was getting into when she married Frank, she proved an ideal wilderness wife. After Frank built the two-story log home on the east side of the Bowron River, it became the center of his guiding and farming operation. In time he built a mill, run by the engine of an old car abandoned in Barkerville. Frank and Anna Kibbee were the first to settle this area, but their example inspired and enthused others and over the next few years several others pre-empted land on Bowron Lake and River.

On May 15, 1913, their first of four children, Juanita, was born. Frank D. Kibbee Jr. was born July 8, 1917, but tragically died before he was two. Juanita's life was also short. She died at 14. They are both buried in a small family plot on the shores of

Bowron Lake. Two others, Hazel and Jessie, married and left the Cariboo. In 1918 the family moved to Barkerville to a house Frank skidded uptown in 1917. It is now a prime example of Cariboo add-on architecture.

When Bowron Lake was made a Game Reserve in 1926, Kibbee became a game warden, a position he held for many years through many adventures. In the 1940s, after Anna died, Frank moved to Vancouver to be near his daughter, Hazel Sturenburg. His adventure-filled life ended there soon after, at age 83.

Floyd deWitt Reed

Howard Harris in *Ten Golden Years* says "Big Reed" was one of the best known and well liked guides on the lakes. A big friendly man who ran an efficient hunting and trapping operation, Reed was born in Washington County, Ohio, but spent most of his life in the Cariboo.

In 1913 he pre-empted 64 ha (159 acres) on the north end of Bowron Lake where the government campsite and registration centre are now located. In 1921, when Bowron residents were busy trying to farm their land, Reed hired B. Parsons and J. Rivers to clear 24 ha (60 acres) for him. By 1926, Reed had been joined by another Ohioan named Morris, and they were trying to "...get their seed in for early germination."

Reed loved the mountains. He once crossed to Tete Jaune Cache via the Cariboo River and went in search of a legendary lost gold mine on Mount Robson. He was also a proponent of the Goat River Road, which he optimistically called the Bowron Lake-Fraser River Highway, a transcontinental route he felt would see the Bowron Lake district attract tourists the same as Jasper.

Like many Bowron residents, Reed also had a home in Barkerville. He bought what is known as the Van Volkenburg cabin on Front Street from the Sam Roger's estate. In 1922 he was making "...extensive alterations to his residence.... The improvements present a magnificent appearance and are a credit to our local architect." Unfortunately, Reed's magnificent alterations, a bay window and siding, in today's Barkerville have been removed to bring the cabin to an earlier appearance.

Reed married in the summer of 1932, at age 44. In November his wife took him to the hospital with a heart attack. He seemed to be recovering, but on November 15, Reed died.

The Wendles

One of the men Frank Kibbee introduced to the Bowron Lake chain was Joe Wendle. He arrived in the Cariboo in 1895, about the same time as Kibbee. Joe was born April 17, 1871, in Kansas, one of eight children. When his father died in 1884, 13-year-old Joe left home. For 17 years the family heard nothing of him. Wendle came to British Columbia to work for the Canadian Pacific Railway in its exploration for coal deposits. One was in the Cariboo and here Joe was attracted to the Bowron country. He worked for several mining companies while developing prospects and interests of his own. He was involved in the Guyet and the La Fontaine mines and had claims on Cunningham Creek. With Beech LaSalle and John Bowron, he worked the Hard-Up claim on Grouse Creek, with some success.

Sometime before he renewed contact with his family in 1901, Joe married Elizabeth Knowles in Perth, Ontario. They stayed in Victoria for some time before moving to Barkerville where they lived in a home Beech Lasalle and Wendle had built, still known as the Wendle House.

On January 21, 1909, Joe became a Canadian citizen. Nine months later he pre-empted 107 ha (266 acres) at the north end of Bowron Lake, west of the river. Here Joe and Betty established a lodge and home, completed in the winter of 1915-16. Their home burned down April 28, 1921, when a spark from the chimney lodged on the shake roof. Betty was home alone with Mrs. Armstrong when the fire occurred and all that could be saved was a gramophone and a bear skin rug. A large number of skins were lost and a valuable player piano.

Betty Wendle's prowess with a rifle was legendary, as the pelts on the walls and floors of the Barkerville home indicate. In one oft-told incident, the Wendles were out hunting on Slide Mountain when suddenly a grizzly stood up right in front of her. She quickly fired and saw it fall, then rise again. She fired a second time, and it fell again. When Joe caught up to her she announced. "I've shot a bear." To their surprise, she had shot two.

The Wendles also recognized a small lake just north of Barkerville on the Bowron Road as a potential recreation site. They built change houses, stocked it with fish, encouraged the wild flowers with care and replanting, and eventually had it declared a park. The lake, now Wendle Lake Provincial Park, is named for them, as is Betty Wendle Creek on the east side of Isaac Lake. In 1958, shortly before his death, Joe Wendle was presented with a Certificate of Merit by the Lieutenant-Governor and the Premier of British Columbia for his contributions to the Barkerville-Bowron Lake community.

The Wendles had no children. Joe died May 18, 1963, at 92, at which time Betty moved to Quesnel. She died there in January 1973.

Joe and Betty Wendle and their first home on Bowron Lake.

Top: George Turner's pack outfit at Bowron Lake. For decades canoes and horses were the summer transportation methods on the lakes.

36

George, Wyn and Mary Turner

George F. Turner was born in Toronto in 1871, the son of a carpet merchant. It was not an occupation George wanted, so at 14 he apprenticed as midshipman in the British merchant marine. He remained in the service for nine years, served on Great Lakes steamships for five years and then with the sealing fleet in the Bering Sea.

After leaving shipboard life at 28, Turner went to the Porcupine mining area of northern Ontario with his uncle, H. T. Windt, a Cariboo miner and rancher at Alexandria near Quesnel.

Likely following Windt's suggestion, Turner came to the Cariboo in 1898 and worked for various mining companies. His eastern-born wife, Winnifred, or Wyn, joined him. He became mine superintendent for Lester Bonner at the West Canadian Deep Lead Mine in Little Valley and they lived on Nelson Creek. Wyn's brother, Robert, came to work for Bonner, and her sister often visited.

The lakes were a popular playground for Barkerville residents and often the Bonners would set out with Frank Kibbee and his first wife, Emma, for a hunting or fishing expedition. Wyn was evidently a popular lady, a fine shot and a great sport. A family history says she was "...tall and always slender. She had a neat face and fair hair. She was vivacious, with a ready tongue and considerable wit."

In 1910 Wyn left George. In 1915 he joined up with the 67th Battalion of Western Scots to serve in World War One. In France he received a serious leg wound and was sent to England to recuperate. George and Wyn evidently married again soon after he returned, but they quickly divorced. "It was something not discussed in the family," say letters. Wyn married Jack MacPherson of Stanley in 1920 and died in 1947.

While recuperating in England, George had met Mary Bradley. When Wyn and he divorced he sent for Mary. They were married in Vancouver in the summer of 1920 and a year later had a daughter, Margaret.

The Turners were now living at Bowron Lake. George had always liked the area and built a large home on acreage he bought from Kenneth McLeod, originally pre-empted by Frank Kibbee. The Turner house was just north of the present Bear River Mercantile.

For a while Turner was in the B.C. Provincial Police and later became game warden for the Bowron Lake area. He died in Barkerville in 1938, a victim of the wound he had received overseas. His wife Mary died in 1969.

The Thompson Brothers

Roy and Norman Thompson arrived in the Bowron Lake country early in the 1900s. They had stumbled on the lakes some years earlier while surveying for a proposed railway, and came to trap and farm. Fred Ludditt says Roy arrived in 1907, on his way to stake timber leases for a large Canadian company on the Upper Fraser River. Norman arrived in 1910 by bicycle from Ashcroft to Quesnel.

By 1913 they were recognized trappers on Bear River. In January 1916, Norman pre-empted 64 ha (158 acres) on a small lake, at that time called Beaver, now Thompson, that sits like a blister on the north side of Kibbee Lake. Their trapline ran north toward Kruger Lake.

While out on their trapline one winter, they found they were not going to reach their cabin, so sheltered in Al Littlefield's who was away. They made themselves at home, which included pouring a couple of stiff shots of rum. When Littlefield returned the next day the Thompsons were lying sick in the bunks, sure they were going to die. Apologetically, Littlefield explained he had doctored the rum to teach a borrowing neighbor a good lesson. Both survived and signed up for service in World War One.

In 1921 Norman married Pearl Roddick, daughter of Ellie and John Roddick who came to Barkerville about 1897. Norman built a home east of the Bowron River. According to Jean Speare in Bowron Chain of Lakes, this home burned down in the 1950s while rented to Federal Fisheries to house summer students. Norman and Pearl later moved into Barkerville so their children could attend school and lived in the old Royal Cariboo Hospital.

Norman and Roy tried raising marten and fisher, but the fisher wouldn't breed and the marten ate their young. They then turned to big-game guiding and operated from 1922 to 1932 from their lodge on Bowron Lake. They discontinued this operation when the lodge burned down. Norman also kept a few pack horses in Barkerville for packing miners into remote claims.

In 1930 Roy married Ellen (Nell) Newton, a woman he had met in Scotland during the war. Nell and Roy were married in Vancouver, but when they reached Barkerville they were treated to a rousing reception and then a grand ball at the Theatre Royal. In the Barkerville tradition, the celebration ended at dawn.

For a while the couple took over the dining room at the Nicol Hotel, but most of their time was spent at the Bowron Lake home. In December 1942, Roy kissed his wife goodbye, said, "I'll see you at Christmas," and headed out for his trap line.

When Roy didn't return, Game Warden Ernie Holmes set out to search and follow what he thought would have been Thompson's route to town from the trapline. Crossing Kruger Lake, Holmes found a hat sitting on the ice, and snowshoe tracks that ended abruptly. He was convinced he had found Roy Thompson. He returned a few days later with local men, including Fred Becker and Ole Nelson. By dragging through holes they chopped in the ice they retrieved Thompson's body and buried him beside the lake. He was one of many trappers killed by treacherous ice conditions.

Nell Thompson became Barkerville postmistress, married Ted Dowsett two years later and remained postmistress until 1964. Norman and Pearl then moved to Quesnel where Norman died in 1968.

The Thompson trapline was sold to Paul Pavich, for whom Pavich Island in Swan Lake is named.

George "Scotty" Gilchrist

Gilchrist was little more than a teenager when he arrived in 1908, from Hawick, Scotland. By 1914 he had pre-empted 54 ha (133 acres) on Indianpoint Creek, later the home of the McCabes. The paperwork, however, wasn't even completed when he signed up with several other Barkerville and Quesnel boys in the 54th Battalion to serve in World War One.

Harry and Tom Brierley, trappers who had a cabin on Wolverine Bay in 1912, were there, along with Mickey Mercer, Charlie Evans, Clyde Kepner, Jack Ellis and two of the Boyd brothers, both of whom were killed.

In July 1917 he was a sergeant at the Cite De Moulin battle and wrote that during the battle he heard a shell burst. "The man next to me was killed. Another lost an arm and I could hear him shouting 'where is my arm' and I shouted back 'where is my arse.' I thought it was blown off! I got pieces in the legs, hips and arms, but otherwise I am feeling okay."

Gilchrist recuperated in hospital and at his parents home in Scotland. It seems he married at this time to "Jeanie," but she stayed in Scotland when he returned to the Bowron country. He joined the Forestry Department and worked on the lakes. His sister, Jean, followed him to Barkerville in 1920.

About the same time, Scotty built a home in Barkerville. In 1923 he suffered an accident while on patrol, resulting in a long illness. When he died May 17, 1931, his assets were a lot in Quesnel and some cash, for a total of $1,687.56. He left his wife, "Jeanie Gilchrist, of Glasgow, Scotland, living under the name Mrs. Kinnon, the sum of $1.00, and no more."

The McCabes

The natural wilderness beauty of Bear Lake attracted people other than guides, trappers and hunters. Some were introduced by guides such as Kibbee and Wendle, while others found their own way in. Thomas and Eleanor McCabe were two such people.

Following World War One, the McCabes were searching for a natural haven where they could settle. Aboard a boat travelling from Vancouver to Prince Rupert, they chanced to meet Major Motherwell of the Dominion Fisheries. "Go to Bear Lake," the Major said when he learned of their quest. "Go to Bear Lake and your fate is sealed. There is no place like it."

The McCabes followed Motherwell's advice and a short time later bounced over the rough road west from Quesnel some 115 km (70 miles) to Bear Lake. Their story, left to us in newspaper clippings written in the mid 1930s by Louis Le Bourdais, illustrates the feelings and life style of another group of Bowron Lake aficionados.

"On Indian Point Lake," Le Bourdais wrote, "a retired Imperial army officer, still a young man, has built a wonderful log camp, fitted it up with a stone fireplace and furnished it elaborately and comfortably, with rustic furniture, home-made but splendidly fashioned, and with chairs in old colonial style, brought all the way from the New England states.

"An artist's easel occupies a prominent position in the big living-room, for the owner is a painter of no mere ability. Before the war, this officer, who is a New Englander, was a member of the faculties of Harvard, Yale and the United States naval academy, teaching literature and history. His wife, who came from Cambridge, a descendant of a very old New England family, had always lived the more or less luxurious life of the well-born which included several years spent in travel abroad. Yet she and her husband are not only content to spend the summer months in camp and upon the lakes and mountains, which entails quite a considerable amount of hardship even for one accustomed to this sort of life, especially the mountain climbing, many peaks being over 7,000 feet, but they spend some winters there as well. Each spring before the breakup, with a light canoe lashed upon a toboggan, they strike out across the chain of lakes, their objective the highest pinnacle of some uncharted peak beyond Isaac's Lake, outside the parallelogram, or perhaps one of the many that rear their rocky crags in serried ranks within its borders.

"Long before their return to the main camp at Indian Point, the snowshoes and the sled would have given place to paddle and canoe.

"A more versatile couple it would be hard to find than this officer and his wife. They are as much at home in a canoe on a rough 'sea' on Isaac's Lake, on shore, with a double-bitted axe, or on the trail with a stubborn pack-horse (they can throw the diamond hitch blindfolded), as they would be in the art galleries of the Louvre.

"'We stay here, not because we have to, but because we think there's no place like it,' said the former world traveller, 'and the only reason there aren't more people like ourselves here is because they don't know there is such a place.'"

The McCabes actually had two homes. The one on Indianpoint Lake was originally pre-empted by George Gilchrist in 1914. The second was on 9.7 ha (25 acres) on the west shore of Bowron Lake, near the Kibbees, purchased from the Crown in 1924. They were keen naturalists and kept detailed notes of animal and bird life. In 1925 McCabe was one of those who convinced the government of B.C. to establish a game reserve.

After living here for a number of years the McCabes separated. Thomas became a professor at the University of California. Eleanor continued to visit their Indianpoint Lodge for many years, but eventually the sojourns became less frequent. Finally, the property was taken over by Provincial Parks. In a moment of pyromaniac enthusiasm to return the land to wilderness, the lodge along with its library and furniture was torched. Canoeists can still visit the remains, marked by a lonely stone chimney on the north shore of Indianpoint Lake.

The Cochrans

James Dean Cochran and Lutie Ulrich Cochran came from Oregon in 1912, shortly after they were married. The following autumn he pre-empted 65 ha (160 acres) on Indianpoint Creek, 29 km (18 miles) down the Bowron River, where they built a house, stables and corrals.

The Cochrans were avid promoters of the country. In 1913 the *Cariboo Observer* reported that "Mr. Cochran is very enthusiastic over the prospects of the Lower Bear River country for mixed farming and informs us that several of his former neighbors in Oregon intend coming out during the summer with the intention of locating in that section."

Dean and Lutie became active big-game guides in the mountains to the north where a peak is named for them. They had one son, Ulrich, and moved to Barkerville for his schooling. Dean died in the 1950s and Lutie moved to Quesnel, but continued to spend summers in Barkerville.

Lutie wrote a book about their early Indianpoint days, *The Wilderness Told Me*, which has become a local classic.

Becker's Lodge

In 1931, following the lead of the Kibbees, Wendles and McCabes, an American from Nevada decided to establish an exclusive hunting and fishing lodge on Bowron Lake. Grover Youngs selected a site on a high bluff overlooking the length of the lake and with six men built a lodge and two cabins. They used only hand tools — a peavy, crosscut saw, axe and maul.

The walls and rafters were built of local spruce but the original cedar shake roof came from shake bolts brought from Sandy Lake. It took three weeks to select the trees, cut them into bolts and then build a raft 2 m (6 feet) by 23 m (70 feet). During the trip the raft had to be disassembled three times and the bolts portaged between lakes.

Originally named the Cariboo Hunting and Fishing Lodge, it has been in continuous operation since 1934, the hardwood floors the original ones. The Youngs sold to Colonel and Mrs. Parker, also Americans, and the Parkers to Eleanor Crump and Stan Ross. They in turn sold to Frank and Ruth Cushman who also came from the U.S.A.

The Cushmans ran the lodge until 1969 when they sold to Fred and Dodie Becker who changed the name to Becker's (no relation to old Fred Becker, the McLeary Lake trapper). Since then the Lodge has changed hands several times and is currently owned by Lothar Vollmer.

The Cushmans

Frank Cushman served as a U.S. Marine in the Pacific campaign during World War Two and then spent a few years in college and working for the U.S. Forest Service. He and his wife, Ruth, decided to see what the country north was like, and owned a small ranch in the Kamloops area. But after coming to the Cariboo and operating the Cariboo Hunting and Fishing Lodge, the Cushmans were hooked on the Bowron country and moved only a few miles away to the Bowron River where with the help of son, Tim, Frank continued his guiding business.

Frank Cushman, like Frank Kibbee, has a Bowron Lake grizzly story. On October 29, 1975, Frank went to his Kruger Lake cabin to prepare it for hunting parties. As a precaution, he grabbed a rifle and stuck a few cartridges in his belt.

At the cabin he realized something wasn't quite right. Then, from around the corner of the cabin, a brown blur charged. Grizzly. Cushman jacked a cartridge into his rifle and fired from the hip. He saw the bullet hit and hair fly, but the bear kept coming. He chambered another shell and fired — and missed. By this time the bear was on top of him. As Frank backed into the lake he stumbled and fell, the bear charging in after him.

The grizzly was now on all fours, wading to where Cushman lay on his back, struggling to chamber another round. He worked the bolt again, aimed at the bear's head now only a couple of feet away, and pulled the trigger. Click. Misfire.

The bear looked at Cushman, staggered, and fell beside him in the lake's cold water. Cushman's first bullet, he later discovered, had hit the bear's heart, but the momentum and adrenalin of the charge carried it forward. What was more surprising was that the cartridges were for a different rifle. Cushman had chambered 7mm rounds into a .300 Winchester Magnum. The bullet had spun down the barrel and, fortunately, tumbled into the short-range target.

Frank Cushman welded the bullet on his belt buckle, a reminder to always check his load.

Frank and Ruth have retired to Cottonwood where Old Ephriam, as he was dubbed, stands in rigid charge in the Cushman's home. Tim and his wife, Judy, continue guiding in the Bowron country, in summer with horses and in winter by dog team.

The McKitricks

Bowron Lake Lodge, unlike Becker's, has changed ownership only once during the several decades it has been in operation. The 107-ha (266-acre) parcel on which the lodge now stands was pre-empted by Joe Wendle in 1909. The Wendles built a lodge and a home as the base of his guiding operation. The home burned down in 1924, but a lodge he built in 1933 he sold to Bill McKitrick in 1935.

The McKitrick family, Bill and Kezia and sons Arnold, Harold and Roy, came from Vancouver, an exception to the usual Americans inhabiting the lakes.

McKitrick expanded the operations to include a sawmill, traplines, a ranch, cabins, canoe rentals and an airstrip. Bill McKitrick died in 1959 and his wife in 1986.

After Bill died his son, Roy, took over the operation with his wife Kitty. Now their sons have a hand in the operation.

Trappers, Hunters and Farmers

There were many others who drifted in and out of the Bowron Lake country, leaving few reminders of their passage. James Duffey, for instance. He came to Barkerville in 1887, at age 17. In 1915 he pre-empted 38 ha (94 acres) 10 km (6 miles) down the Bowron River. He trapped, prospected and guided, and was welcomed at Barkerville dances as a fine piano player. Many trappers used his cabin as a stopping point.

In May 1939 after he had been missing for a month, Joe Wendle went looking for him. He was found under a spruce tree three miles from his cabin. While loading his boat he had mis-fired his rifle and shot himself.

The Anderson brothers, Maurice and John, were Norwegians who trapped the lakes with a cabin at Atlas Lake. When Tom Brierley moved to Vancouver Island, Maurice bought his Bark-erville house and moved in. John died in 1924 but Maurice was still wandering the country in the early 1950s.

Harold Mason was a driller for a Barkerville mining com-pany. He married in 1925 and built a fine home on Bowron Lake. The Masons made the paper in October 1926 when a black bear broke into the house and laid waste to the interior. Noted the local paper: "Barkerville people think this must have been the pet bear 'Topsy' which Mrs. Murphy turned loose at Cochran's headquarters on Indian Point Creek last fall. Topsy was always full of mischief, and would be just cute enough to know that Mason's cabin is located just inside the game sanctuary."

The Mason home wasn't finished with ill fortune. It slid into the lake during a landslide in the 1930s.

Trapper Fred Becker came to Barkerville with his brother, Otto, in 1932 to work on the electrical plant at the Cariboo Gold Quartz Mine in Wells. He then established the first light plant in Barkerville. Though it brought electric light to the town for the first time, it was not financially successful and Fred went to work for Island Mountain Mine.

Becker became part of the Bowron story when he decided to short circuit his career and take up trapping and big-game guid-ing. His trap line centered out of McLeary Lake. In later years his hobbies of painting and photography came to the fore, his guiding trips providing him with a multitude of subjects. When Fred and his wife left Bowron and Barkerville they settled in Kamloops.

Henry Rivers was "a soft-spoken French-Canadian" who in 1921 pre-empted about 65 ha (160 acres) 6 km (10 miles) down the Bowron River. In the early 1930s he died on the trail.

And then there was Ernest Hilton Livingstone, a miner who told the census enumerator that his religion was as a "Free Thinker." In 1901 he was living with James Robinson, an English miner. We know little about him, but in 1907 he was a Bear Lake trapper. One September he was visiting an Indian woman, with bottle in hand and likely passion in mind. It was a common occurrence in the mining camps. But something went wrong and he was charged with killing an Indian.

Frank Kibbee and one of the Thompson brothers gave evi-dence for the prosecution in a Richfield police court. No verdict

Frank Cushman in the role of gold-rush miner
Ned Stout during Barkerville's summer season.

was rendered and Livingstone was committed to Kamloops jail.
There his story ends. He did not appear on the docket at the next
two assizes and he appears in no other records or newspapers
that have surfaced. His ultimate guilt or innocence remains
another mystery of the Bowron Lake country.

Chapter Three
Natural History

Geology

In Precambrian times more than 600 million years ago, mud and sand were deposited in a sea lying on the continental margin of the Canadian Shield. These early deposits are referred to as the Kaza Group. Over millions of years the Kaza deposits reached a depth of over 3,300 m (10,000 feet).

As conditions in the sea, and materials being eroded from the continental land mass changed during the Cambrian period (440-600 million years ago), the layers of sediment varied, forming a second layer of rock called the Cariboo Group. This group consists of seven sequences of rock, three of which are exposed along the shores of the lake chain.

The Isaac Formation shows along the east side of Isaac Lake, south of Betty Wendle Creek to a point some 3.2 km (2 miles) north of the south end of the lake. The younger Cunningham Formation is found along the east side of Isaac Lake, north of Betty Wendle Creek.

The Mural Formation is the youngest and crops out along the east shores of Spectacle Lakes and the west and south shores of Indianpoint Lake. It is limestone and contains fossils of trilobites and primitive corals.

The third group of rocks in the park are the sedimentary and volcanic Slide Mountain Group, about 250 million years old. It is formed of the Antler Formation, exposed on the hills to the southwest and northeast of Bowron Lake, and the Guyet Foundation which crops out on a small island called the Bowler Hat at the north end of Swan Lake.

One hundred million years after the depositing of sediments, the various strata were subjected to great heat and pressure and underwent deformation, metamorphism and uplifting. These processes, and 100 million years of erosion, have removed overlying younger formations and shaped the present form of the Cariboo Mountains.

The physical features of the park as we see them today are a result of the structures formed during mountain building. The unusual alignment of the ridges and valleys are a result of folding, faults and erosion.

Imagine the layers of sediment laid down on the seabed as a multi-layered carpet. Push the carpet together from both sides

There are some 160 different birds in the Bowron region, with others yet to be identified. (See checklist on page 122.)

Among the known ones are the Canada goose and that friendly symbol of the wilderness, the Canada jay. The dipper, above, feeds on the bottom of streams, constantly bobbing up and down, hence its name.

47

and ridges and valleys will form. The upraised ridges are termed "anticlines," and the valleys, or troughs, are "synclines." An example of an anticline is the crest that runs from the west end of Isaac Lake to Lanezi Lake. The synclines on either side are the main arm of Isaac Lake and Bowron-Spectacle Lakes. This ridge, however, is cut by the valleys of Bowron River and Pomeroy, Hucky and Harold Creeks. These valleys are fractures in the anticlines crest. Fractures or cracks in the earth's crust during the late stages of fold formation can be oriented in two directions: parallel to the anticline, or at right angles to the anticline. If movement takes place along a fracture it is termed a fault. Faults and fractures are weak zones and erosion is more rapid, resulting in fractures and faults often being occupied by water courses. So now imagine our carpet fold eroded to expose various layers, and cracking at right angles to the ridge. The cracks are the creeks previously named, as well as Kibbee Lake and Lanezi Lake. Cracks, and then faulting parallel to the ridge, are the Isaac Lake Valley and the Bowron-Spectacle Lakes Valley.

But formation of the terrain we see today did not stop 100 million years ago. Since then other changes have occurred. The lake circuit includes two of the major physiographic divisons of British Columbia — the Quesnel Highlands in the west and the Cariboo Mountains in the east. The Quesnel Highlands are characterized by summit elevations of 1,600 to 2,100 m (5,250 to nearly 7,000 feet). The mountains are broad and rounded and form a transition zone from the low elevations of the Interior Plateau to the Cariboo Mountains. The rugged Cariboo Mountains have summits over 2,100 m (7,000 feet), with cirques and cirque glaciers common.

These forms were altered beginning in the Cretaceous period 60 million years ago when the major drainage channels of British Columbia were formed. The transformation continued through the Eocene time until approximately 25,000 years ago when glacial conditions covered most of the province in ice. Valleys filled with ice that moved outwards, eventually covering the Cariboo Mountains. This ice sheet was nearly static at its center but active toward its margin, with an average elevation about 2,000 m (6,600 feet).

The Quesnel Highlands were eroded in a different manner to the Cariboo Mountains. They were completely over-ridden by moving ice, thus the rolling upland plateau surface was produced. On the other hand, the Cariboo Mountains glaciation created sharp ridged, steep-walled valleys and extensive cirques. Glacial till covers the lower slopes and large boulders termed "glacial erratics" are common on the lake shores. Several small glaciers in the park and the surrounding mountains are reminders of this frigid past.

As the glaciers retreated about 12,000 years ago, drainage patterns changed. The Cariboo River was blocked by till and ice and water flowed north via the Indianpoint Valley, creating the delta evident today. When the retreating glacier's terminus was in the Sandy Lake area, dry strong winds blowing off the ice formed loess deposits and sand dunes in the Sandy and Babcock Lakes area. From Sandy to the Spectacle Lakes is a kettled outwash plain, deposits of stratified gravels left by meltwater streams. Unna Lake is likely a kettle — a depression formed when a large pocket of glacial ice, buried in the plain, melted.

This land formed by so many varied processes over the last millions of years is the parallelogram which now offers canoeists a chain of lakes and rivers through a textbook course in the earth's formation.

The Plants

Bowron Lake Park is for the most part in what is termed the Sub-alpine Forest Zone, characterized by being above 1,150 m (3,500 feet) with a predominance of spruce and balsam trees. There are sections, however, which more closely resemble the Interior Wet Belt with its fir, cedar and hemlock. Plants from both zones occur in various areas of the park which, with its mountains, also includes the Alpine area zone.

As well as the trees which form the dominent cover, there are shrubs and berries such as twinberry, false box, kinnikinnick, Labrador tea, cranberry, huckleberry, mountain ash, red-osier dogwood, soopolallie, white rhododendron, sticky current and many others.

Flowers blooming from the forest floor through a water-side environment to the alpine include the arnicas, false azalea, bunchberry, cinquefoil, cotton grass, erigonums, Solomon's seal, several species of fireweed, foam flower, asters, pussy-toes, eight species of equisetum, or horsetail, oak-fern, lady fern, stinging nettle, smartweed, spring beauty, water lily, western anemone, columbine, marsh marigold, buttercups, many species of the saxifrage family, spireas, violets, sarsaparilla, cow parsnip, Indian paintbrush, plantains, honeysuckle, northern bedstraw, harebell, goldenrod, Queen's cup, glacier lily, lily-of-the-valley, twisted stalk, hellebore, calypso bulbosa, coralroot, lady's-slipper, tall white bog-orchid and ladies' tresses, to name only a few.

The Mammals

Because Bowron Lake Provincial Park has been a game sanctuary for over half a century, paddlers are more likely to see wildlife than in settled areas. It is a popular place for those wanting to photograph animals, although the animals canoeists are most likely to see are those that inhabit aquatic environments, such as moose. Deer are sometimes seen around Unna Lake and the west side, and bears are found throughout. Other large mammals such as caribou, mountain goats and grizzly bears inhabit alpine areas and thus are not usually seen. The smaller mammals of the park, with the exception of beaver, otter and perhaps mink, are seldom seen. Fisher, wolverine, mink, weasel, cougar and other members of the cat family are secretive mammals, mainly nocturnal, and usually leave only tracks.

Although bears should be treated with caution, as described elsewhere, there is no need to approach the Bowron chain with fear. You will likely hear lots of bear stories, as early pioneers heard Indian stories, but in most cases they will be exaggerated, and one incident told many times becomes several incidents. There are two bears common to the Bowron chain.

The black bear is the smallest member of the *Ursus* family in North America, the most widely distributed and will be found on all parts of the chain. Contrary to what their name implies, pelts are not always black but can vary through cinnamon and blonde to the white Kermode of the B.C. coast. Though they are the smallest bear, they still range from 56-270 kg (125-600 pounds), males tending to be larger than females. They prefer wooded areas but can be found almost anywhere. Creatures of habit, neither sociable nor gregarious, they prefer their own solitary company. Black bears den up for part of the winter but are not true hibernators as their body temperature remains normal.

Their omnivorous foraging for food is done mostly at night. It is usually in areas unfrequented by humans that they are seen moving around in daylight hours. Because they are creatures of habit, a mother can teach a youngster to check campsites or packs for food, beginning a behavior pattern that is difficult to break. For this reason, be sure to use caches. Take the suggested precautions to protect not only yourself but those following.

Although the magnificent grizzly has become an endangered species with some sub-species even extinct in areas of the continent, there is still a good population in British Columbia. The Bowron country is part of their range, in particular the higher alpine area and the Bowron River in the autumn salmon-spawning time.

Adult grizzlies can weigh from 200-450 kg (450-1,000 pounds). At times it may be difficult to distinguish a small grizzly from a large cinnamon-colored black bear but the grizzly

The two large mammals most likely to be seen by visitors are mule deer and moose. Although coyotes are year-round residents, they are secretive, seen mostly in winter when the lakes are frozen.

does have distinguishing characteristics, including: a dished or concave face, prominent muscular hump over the shoulders and long curved claws. Its coat can vary from black to blonde and is often "grizzled," or tipped with silver. These large bears migrate from valley bottoms to alpine areas in the summer. They are hunters, fishers and powerful swimmers. Like blacks they den up in winter but are not true hibernators.

The ungulates of the park include mountain goats, caribou, deer and moose. As already noted, paddlers are most likely to see moose and mule deer.

Moose, in fact, might well be the symbol of Bowron Lake Provincial Park. Of all large mammals, they are the most commonly seen. Like the bison of the prairies, they are extremely well adapted to their environment. Strong jaws easily snap off twigs and adeptly pluck aquatic plants from pond bottoms. Long slim legs supported on widely spread cloven hooves allow easy travel through tangled windfall and soft bogs alike. Senses are developed in tune with their habitat. While their eyesight is poor, their sense of smell and hearing is acute.

In Europe, moose have been used as draft animals for centuries. Domestication, in fact, has a long history. In the Middle Ages the community of Dorpat, Esthonia, forbade riding moose on city streets. Catherine the Great kept them under strict government control to prevent them being used as mounts by rebellious tribesmen and prisoners escaping the frozen wastes of Siberia. Guards riding horses were at a great disadvantage if moose riders headed for the natural habitat of swamps and bogs.

While moose may be seen almost anywhere on the lakes, the most likely area is the Bowron Marsh and the shallow northern end of Swan Lake. In autumn they can sometimes be heard calling for many miles, a surprising rush of grunts, groans and bellows. Although they are relatively harmless, canoeists are cautioned to keep away to avoid any possibility of an upset cow with calf charging and upsetting a canoe.

Mule deer are the most widespread of the deer family in the province, and the only species in Bowron Park. They are distinguishable by their large mule-like ears, black-tipped tail and distinctive, branched antlers on the male through fall and early winter. (Like moose, they shed their antlers every year.) Their sharp alert senses and agility are of special importance since they are a key prey for large predators such as cougars and wolves. The critical survival time for deer, as with most wildlife, is winter when maximum energy is required and minimum nutrition is available. It is most important when animals are in this crucial period that they should not be harassed in any way. Even a skier can stress an animal to a point where its lack of reserve energy will not allow it to recover.

Mountain caribou, the large member of the deer family for which the Cariboo region is named, frequent the alpine regions surrounding the lakes. They are, therefore, seldom seen except during spring and fall migrations. They are large deer-like mammals with a distinctive trotting gait, semi-palmated antlers and an inquisitive nature. Unlike other members of the deer family, both sexes of caribou may have antlers. They are fast runners and good swimmers, and migrate between summer and winter ranges. As browsers, caribou depend to a great extent on lichens for winter food. The main problems endangering caribou as a group are interference in their migration routes and loss of wintering ranges and food to man's encroachment, specifically high altitude logging.

Mountain goats, the mammal the color of winter, are another seldom-seen, high-country animal. The mountain goat is technically better described as a goat-antelope — in fact, its closest relative is the chamois of the Alps. The goat really doesn't fit into any of the families we recognize. Like elk, deer and moose, it is an even-toed ungulate. But like the prairie pronghorn antelope, it is hollow horned and, finally, belongs to the same sub-family as the musk-ox and mountain sheep.

Since few fossils remains have been found, the evolution of the goat is poorly understood. It is thought that they arrived during the early Pleistocene, more than 100,000 years ago, via a land bridge across Bering Strait. The oldest known remains were found only a few miles south of Bowron Lake in 1932 when hydraulic miners unearthed a skull and horncores under 83 m (275 feet) of gold-bearing sediment at the Bullion Pit Mine near Quesnel Forks. They were estimated to be more than 100,000 years old.

Although the goat is often confused with the bighorn sheep — not present in this area — the goat's white coat, short black horns and blocky shape distinguish it from sheep. Goats are generally considered to be non-migratory and inhabit the roughest possible terrain in mountain ranges. Food consists of a variety of plants from alpine flowers to any tree except spruce. They are most likely to be seen in the high alpine crags along Isaac Lake.

Another smaller mammal of importance to the Bowron region from a historic — if not a modern — perspective is the beaver. This large rodent was responsible, more than anything else, for the early exploration and development of New Caledonia, later the province of British Columbia. For centuries the pelt of the beaver dominated the fur trade and was the reason for the

To discourage black bears from visiting campsites, canoeists should never leave food sitting around or in tents, but use the protected caches.

birth of the Hudson's Bay Company, which for centuries held a monopoly over most of present-day Canada. Fashionable fur hats and the market for good pelts resulted in a whole continent being explored and exploited.

This exploitation resulted in the beaver becoming practically extinct in many areas of North America. Even in the lifetime of Alexander Mackenzie there was a noticeable decline in the number of pelts being traded. As one area was stripped of beaver, the posts and forts advanced further and further into the wilderness. Eventually, a change in fashions away from the beaver hat made it possible for the beaver to make a gradual comeback. After the Cariboo gold rush opened up the north part of the province and then declined, it was the furbearers that brought men into this region.

The Birds

The bird life of Bowron Park is immensely varied, a reflection of the many different habitats. Lake travellers will undoubtably meet ravens who can undo pack zippers to steal food, whiskey jacks, or Canada jays, on a similar mission, hear loons calling on still evening waters and, on the smaller lakes, see a variety of waterfowl. Ospreys nest on Spectacle Lakes, whistling swans winter on Sandy Lake and migrating Canada and Snow geese rest and feed. The Bowron River estuary is the major area for birders, with many species recorded here.

As the check list in Appendix One indicates, there is a wide variety of birdlife, but to date it has been inadequately documented.

Fish and Fishing

The Bowron and Isaac Lakes drainages are home to a variety of fish species that have for centuries made the lakes popular with anglers from native peoples to today's recreationists. Rainbow, Dolly Varden, kokanee (a land-locked salmon) and Rocky Mountain whitefish are found in most of the lakes, while sockeye and chinook salmon both migrate through the Bowron Lake and Bowron River system.

Sockeye arrive on their Upper Bowron River spawning grounds at the beginning of August, and reach their peak numbers in the first two weeks of September, after swimming upstream for some 1,100 km (700 miles). Like other Fraser River salmon stocks, the Bowron sockeye are cyclical. For this reason, spawners range in number from 2,000 to 35,000. After they emerge from the spawning gravel in spring, juvenile sockeye spend up to two years in the lake before migrating to the sea. These stocks are an important part of the province's commercial fishery. Depending on the cycle, there are 1,200 to 175,000 Bowron fish caught annually.

Chinook salmon spawn outside the park boundary in the Lower Bowron River between Indianpoint Creek and the lake outlet. Some 1,000 to 2,000 spawners yield a catch of about 6,000 to 12,000 per year.

Fishing on the lakes can be fair to excellent, depending on location, season and angling methods. But owing to the uncertain nature of angling, it is recommended that canoeists not rely on catching fish to supplement the usual canoeists' dehydrated foods.

Trolling is the most popular method, with some spin casting and fly fishing. Indianpoint and Isaac Lakes are the most consistent fish producers. Fly-fishing is popular at Hunter Lake, a short hike off Sandy Lake. Rainbow, Dolly Varden, kokanee and Rocky Mountain whitefish are all present. The kokanee run in the late part of June and early July on Bowron Lake is very popular. Winter fishing is good on Kibbee and Indianpoint Lakes. The largest lake trout come from the deep holes in the Wolverine Bay area.

Check with local lodges and stores for the flies and lures that are currently popular.

Chapter Four

Summer on the Lakes

The Chain

Canoeists can paddle the circuit anytime between June and the end of October, sometimes a little earlier. July and August are usually crowded, less so if there is a spell of wet weather, more if the weather turns sunny. Nights will be cool, even in mid-summer. September is a popular month with those who are not tied to summer holidays. Though there will be some cold nights, and perhaps a morning skim of ice on the lakes and water buckets, the deciduous trees are bright in their fall colors, the bugs at a minimum and weather is usually fair. By October, the nights often dip below freezing and ice may form on the lakes.

The usual length of time to complete the circuit is seven to 10 days.

Pre-trip Information

Information on the park can be obtained from Parks Branch District Office in Williams Lake or from the contractor in charge of registrations and reservations. (See addresses in Chapter Ten.)

A copy of an introductory video is available from the contractor with a $24 deposit.

Lodges and Rentals

There are two lodges on Bowron Lake. Both offer accommodation, camping, showers and equipment rentals. It is advisable that you check prices and availability well ahead of your proposed departure.

It is also advisable that you inquire into the equipment being offered. Be sure it suits your needs.

If you are considering hiring a guide, ask for their qualifications and some references.

Supplies

Basic supplies, fishing gear and groceries are available at the lodges and Bear River Mercantile. The nearest gas is in Wells.

Registration

All parties must pre-register and reserve a departure date. The reservation is made through D. J. Park Contractors, 358 Vaughan

Street, Quesnel, B.C. V2J 2T2; phone (604) 992-3111, Fax (604) 992-6624.

Groups, seven to 14 people, including guides and leaders, must register and use only assigned campsites. Groups must have a designated leader responsible for the conduct and actions of all people in the party while in the park. Canoeists may be assigned first night campsites when they make their reservations. This policy is to spread parties over the circuit and avoid the crush when everyone tries to make Wolverine Bay the first night.

There is limited non-reservation, drop-in space available for those who have not planned ahead. A wait of a few days may be necessary.

Fees

A fee is charged for use of the circuit. Fees (1994) are $60 per canoe for the full circuit; $50 for a kayak or single person canoe for full circuit, and $38 per canoe or kayak for the westside only. In 1994 a separate fee will be levied for voyageur type canoes; that is, large canoes with many paddlers. Payment is accepted only in Canadian currency, travellers cheques, Visa or Mastercharge. Personal cheques are not accepted. Remember that fees are subject to change.

Registration Centre

At road's end, adjacent to the parking lot and the campground, there is a registration centre. Displays here show some of the flora and fauna of the park and slide presentations give an introduction. All visitors travelling the circuit must register here in person, pay a user fee, and view the introductory video before embarking. The centre is open June 1 to Labour Day weekend in September, seven days a week, from 7 a.m. to 8 p.m.

Park Facilities

At the beginning of the circuit, near the registration centre, there is a 25-unit campground, including 3 double units, with room for recreational vehicles up to 6 m (20 feet) in length. There are no hookups, but water, pit toilets and firewood are nearby. Campers requiring hookups or showers should check with the lodges.

A small boat-launching site is located at the north end of Bowron Lake and a canoe float a short walk from the campground.

On the circuit there are wilderness campsites with tent pads. Caches for equipment are located at every campsite and portage, as are pit toilets. Toilet paper is not supplied. Caches must be used to prevent any bear problems.

At strategic points large shelters with tables and stoves have been built. Wood is available but you must have your own axe for splitting. The shelters are not meant to be camped in, but as poor-weather havens. Do not sleep in the shelters and be sure to allow room for other campers.

There are eight to 10 old cabins built by trappers and guides in varying stages of repair. While most are open for public use, many are in poor shape. Do not rely on using these cabins as they are sometimes in use by parks staff or other campers, and with each year they come closer to collapsing from winter snow and rot.

Water

Due to the possibility of contracting Beaver Fever, *Giardia Lamblin*, it is recommended that you boil water. Chemical treatment is not as effective as boiling in combating *Giardia.*

Regulations

- Bear caches must be used while camping.

- Power boats are restricted to Bowron Lake only and are not allowed in any part of the Bowron slough.

- Fires are restricted to designated campsites and only in supplied fire rings. Stoves must be used for cooking. Fire bans may be in effect in dry spells.

- Anglers require a valid British Columbia Angling License. They are not available from parks staff but may be purchased at the lodges, in Wells or in Quesnel.

- Firearms are prohibited.

- Garbage and litter — visitors must pack out all garbage.

- Bottles and cans for beverages are banned. This includes all non-alcoholic and alcoholic beverages. Canned soups are allowed.

- Trees, shrubs and flowers are an integral part of the park and their destruction or picking is prohibited.

- The removal of any natural item such as rocks is prohibited.

- Motor vehicles, including motorcycles, ATVs and similar vehicles are restricted to vehicle roads and parking areas.

- Snowmobiles and similar vehicles are prohibited, except with special permission. Violators face confiscation and fines.

- Dogs, cats, domestic pets and horses are prohibited.

- Aircraft entry into Bowron Lake Provincial Park is restricted to Bowron Lake only. Pilots must register at the registration centre.

- While on a cart, canoes cannot be loaded with more than 27 kg (60 pounds). Be prepared to backpack any excess.

Portaging

There are two views on portaging. One is that canoeists are blessed if they do not have to portage; the other that portaging is a welcome break in otherwise endless paddling. On the Bowron Lake circuit the terrain dictates — you portage. The ease of the portage will depend on how prepared your party is for the carry.

In packing, a two-person party should plan on two or three packs at the most — one, or two, with personal gear and the other with food and kitchen equipment. At the portage, the person carrying the canoe hefts the smallest pack and the canoe, while the other takes a heavy pack, axe, perhaps the paddles and, on occasion, the third pack. An alternative is to make two carries — canoe and one pack on the first and two packs on the second. If you have any more than that you have too much gear or food.

Psychologically, it is not a good idea to waste time at the beginning of the portage. Put your excess gear in the cache and go. At the far end of the carry, again use the cache and return for the next load.

Canoe carts, or "wheels," have, unfortunately, become the standard portaging method on the Bowron circuit. They can be rented from either of the lodges. There are two types. Those with inflated bicycle wheels are the best. Paddlers should be aware that these are not the panacea sometimes supposed.

Tires frequently puncture and wheels break under heavy loads or rough use. If the wheels cannot be repaired, paddlers are forced to carry everything, including the wheels, on all portages. It is not uncommon for visitors to plan on using the wheels and pack gear in waterproof boxes. Unfortunately, they make an awkward load in the event of a breakdown.

Do not overload the wheels. Be prepared to pack over all portages. Wheels cause serious wear and tear on trails and a day may come when wheels are banned if canoeists insist on heavy loads.

While there are many ways to carry a canoe, the most common and most effective is for one person to lift and carry. Two people can result in an awkward, jarring, argumentative portage. The canoe is carried with the center thwart across the shoulders. This thwart may be padded or formed into a yoke. If not, paddles can be lashed to the center and rear thwarts, back to front, so that the blades rest on your shoulders. Paddles can be

The Cariboo River where it enters McLeary Lake, the Cariboo Mountains in the background. Since mountains tend to create local weather patterns, winds can arise quickly.

additionally padded with a sweater or personal flotation device.

For novices, lifting a canoe can be a trying experience. The easiest way is to stand at the canoe's side with the interior facing away from you. Grasp the side closest to you, roll the canoe onto your knees and, at the same time, reach across to the far side or to a thwart with one hand, push with your knees and toss the canoe up and over onto your shoulders. This action is not done with slow movement but with a toss. As the canoe reaches head or shoulder height, it should be almost upside down and you will be able to duck your head to the yoke. The canoe should be slightly weighted toward the stern, behind you, so that you can lift the bow to see where you are going.

On the portage trail there are rests where the canoe can be set down with the bow in the air. These rests ensure that you will only have to step underneath to start off again.

Another method of lifting is to have a partner lift the bow of the canoe high in the air while the carrier settles underneath. At the end of the portage the canoe is raised slightly, your head pulled away from the yoke and the canoe lowered to your thighs and then the ground. Many experienced paddlers will arrange this so that one end comes down in the water or, alternatively, will stand in the water while lowering the canoe. By the end of the chain it will all be second nature. As an added bonus, remember that with each camp, your packs become lighter.

Skills and Safety

The lake circuit has been completed by every level of canoeist, from raw beginners to professional paddlers and guides. Paddlers have come off the chain discouraged and elated, injured, wet and stronger. Those who enjoy themselves the most tend to be those who have taken the time to get in shape for 2 km (just over 1 mile) portages, several hours of paddling a day, and who have learned a few basic canoe stokes. The "J" stroke is necessary for the stern paddler to track a straight course and the basic prys, draws and sweeps for river travel. Basic wilderness skills are a necessity. These include using an axe, building a fire in the rain, pitching a proper weather-tight camp and observing weather signs to avoid being caught on the lake in a storm. First-aid and CPR is also a requirement for this type of travel.

Safety precautions include wearing a life jacket or personal flotation device at all times while on the water. Do not overload your canoe. Position your load so your canoe floats level from side to side, with a slight lift to the bow when both paddlers are aboard. Never stand up or change positions while afloat. Tie packs with a rope so that if you capsize the packs will float free, enabling you to right the canoe, but not drifting off or sinking. Stay close to shore and watch for sudden squalls. Although all the large lakes are subject to sudden winds, Isaac Lake is the most likely to bring surprise squalls.

Equipment

Necessary equipment for the trip will include:

- Canoe: Two-person, preferably lightweight.
- Paddles: Three per canoe.
- Rope: 30 m (100 feet) of 5 mm (0.25 inch) for lining.
- Painter: Polypropylene, stern line and bow line for tying up.
- Tent: Waterproof, tested, with mosquito screen.
- Sleeping bag: Warm for cool nights. A fiber fill that retains little moisture when wet is better for canoeing than a down bag.
- Foam mattress: The self-inflating type is compact and comfortable.
- Stove: Fire building is discouraged. Choose a good quality stove that uses naptha or propane. Plan for wet days.
- Axe: 3/4 for splitting firewood for inclement weather.
- Raingear: Good quality pants, jacket, hat.
- Footwear: Light shoes for paddling, boots for hiking or portage.
- Tarpaulin shelter: For storm-bound days and heavy rain.
- Sack: Canvas or burlap for carrying out refuse.
- Hat: Broad-brimmed for rain and sun protection. Warm toque.
- Bug repellent: DEET is the active ingredient, ranging from 25% to 98%. The more the better. Spray repellent is useful for collars and clothing.
- First-aid kit.
- Repair kit: For canoe and paddles.
- Packs: All equipment should be in packs for portaging. Three packs for two people is ideal.
- Toilet paper: Pit toilets are not supplied.
- Flashlight: A lantern is useful in early spring or late fall.
- Aluminum lawn chairs: They may sound excessive, but they are great for old, tired backs at the day's end and may be used to keep packs off the bottom of the canoe and out of bilge water.

Classification of Rivers

The classification of waters according to a grading system is useful as a general guide to their navigability. However, all water bodies are living, moving, changing entities which vary with the weather and the seasons. The standard for grading water is the International River Classification. This standard has limitations since it is based on easy access and egress and average water levels; it does not make allowances for loaded canoes and cold water.

In a wilderness situation the dangers associated with any section of water are increased if help is not available. A stretch of water runnable in a controlled situation may now be unrunnable. For example, an experienced paddler normally capable of handling Grade 3 may only be able to manage Grade 2 with a loaded canoe, where water is cold and help distant. Be aware that a rise or fall in a river's level can alter the grade within a very short time. Although lakes are classified as Grade 1, they can increase with a heavy blow or squall.

The following interpretation of the International River Classification is made by Canoe Sport British Columbia:

Grade 1
Easy. Waves small and regular; passages clear; occasional sand banks and artificial difficulties like bridge piers. Suitable for novices in closed canoes, kayaks and open Canadians.

Grade 2
Quite easy. Rapids of medium difficulty; passages clear and wide. Occasional boulders in stream. Suitable for intermediate paddlers in closed canoes, kayaks and open Canadians.

Grade 3
Medium difficulty. Waves numerous, high, irregular. Rocks and narrow clear passages. Considerable experience in maneuvering required. Advance scouting usually needed. Canoes will ship water, and unless equipped with spray covers, still require frequent emptying. Kayaks must be equipped with spray covers. Suitable for experienced paddlers in closed canoes and kayaks, and expert paddlers in open Canadians.

Grade 4
Difficult. Long rapids, powerful irregular waves; dangerous rocks, boiling eddies; passages difficult to reconnoiter; advance scouting mandatory; powerful and precise maneuvering required. Spray decks mandatory. Suitable for experts in closed canoes and kayaks only. Not suitable for open Canadian canoes.

Grade 5
Very difficult. Extremely demanding long and very violent rap-

ids, following each other almost without interruption. River bed extremely obstructed; big drops; very steep gradient; advance scouting mandatory and usually difficult due to nature of terrain. Suitable for expert paddlers only in closed canoes and kayaks with specific white water training, under expert leadership. Not suitable for open Canadian canoes.

Grade 6
Extraordinarily difficult. The difficulties of Grade 5 carried to extremes. Nearly impossible and very dangerous. Suitable for teams of expert paddlers only in closed boats at favorable water levels and after careful study, with fully trained and experienced rescue teams in position. Not suitable for open Canadian canoes.

Bears and People
Most confrontations between bears and people occur because people interfere with a bear's needs to maintain a territory, to protect offspring, and to satisfy a voracious appetite. For example, people entering wilderness can be threatening a bear's territory or young. Carelessness with food and garbage invites a bear to help itself, leading to problems when it searches for food, when the food is gone, or when it has come to depend on garbage as a food source.

Since many "bear problems" are more correctly "people problems," most incidents can be prevented. When hiking in bear country it is wise to hike in a group and leave your dog at home. Keep in the open where possible and avoid favorite bear food sources such as berry patches and carcasses. In forested areas carry a noisemaker such as a bell. Be on the lookout for bear signs — tracks, droppings, or diggings. If you see a bear, never feed or harass it, or go near a cub. Go out of your way to avoid a black bear. Leave the area at once if there is a grizzly nearby.

Bears are attracted to camps where there is an easy source of food. Food should never be cooked or stored in a tent but kept in one of the caches provided at portages and campsites. Dirty utensils or garbage must be cleaned and put in the cache, as should any unburned garbage. Non-combustibles must be packed out. If you are fishing, wash out your canoe and cache any fish-tainted clothes. Bears may also be attracted by sweet-smelling cosmetics, toothpaste or scented tissues. It is best to leave these in your car, otherwise cache them.

It is impossible to predict how a bear or a human will react to any given situation, but in the case of a bear attack your best chance is to assess your situation and keep calm. (Good luck!) Never run. Experts advise speaking softly and backing slowly out of the bear's territory and toward a large tree which can be climbed. A last resort on being attacked is to play dead, with legs bent up to protect your chest, and hands clasped behind the neck. Or, remember the prayer of the preacher in the song, "The Preacher and the Bear," who said: "Dear Lord if you can't help me, please don't help that grizzly bear."

A knowledge of bears' habits, and careful attention to camp hygiene, are the best ways to avoid any bear problems. Finally, should you encounter an aggressive bear or a camp robber, report the incident to park staff.

Weather

The Bowron Lake chain is a mountain canoe route in the Interior Wet Belt. Therefore it receives mountain weather — unsettled, stormy, with frequent rain. You might canoe in rain for several days, or spend two weeks in brilliant sunshine. Because rain squalls can sneak in suddenly, it is a good idea to travel prepared for wind and rain on even the sunniest day. Loads should be tarped and rain gear stowed in an accessible place. In June and September snow flurries are common and you may well wake to ice on the lake.

Winter travel will depend on suitable weather more than summer travel. The section on winter travel gives more information.

While the long range forecast available at the registration centre may be of some help, you will basically have to take the weather as it comes. However, native people and some modern naturalists do observe a few natural signs which can indicate the weather to expect.

Look for rain if ants disappear; they don't like floods. Birds ruffling their feathers, and oiling themselves portends rain, while seabirds inland means an approaching storm. Squirrels become active before a storm and deer head for open country when the air warns of heavy rain or thunder. Storms are also forecast by crows and gulls gathering, geese flying high and fast, and turtles hiding on pond bottoms.

Early settlers, who did not have the TV weatherman to give satellite photos of weather patterns, made up various rhymes to help warn of fair or foul. The most common is:

"Red sky at night, sailors, delight;
Red sky at morning, sailors take warning."

Another of particular interest to canoeists is:

"When grass is dry at morning light,
Look for rain before the night,
When the grass is dry at night,
Look for rain before the light."

An overturned canoe will do if there is no grass. If it is dry at dawn then look for rain before nightfall. But,

"When the dew is on the grass,
Rain will never come to pass."

Watch your campfire. If smoke hangs low and drifts slowly away, seeking low ground, then rain is due. Voices or canoe paddles might also be heard at a great distance as the barometer drops.

The surest sign of rain? A canoe loaded for a two-week trip.

The cross-draw is an intermediate stroke useful in flowing water.

Chapter Five
Winter on the Lakes

Winter on the Bowron Lake circuit is a time of silence and solitude. While summer months are busy and crowded, winter brings a blanket of quiet, broken by only a few cross-country skiers, winter fisherfolk and occasional snowshoers. Winter allows us to see the lakes at a time when, historically, the circuit was most travelled — by dog sledding packers and snowshoeing trappers. Because there is little change in elevation, the skiing is usually relatively easy, although to some this condition also makes it boring. However, a spring thaw, severe storm, open water or deep snow can all effect a change that will make travel almost impossible.

Parks Branch personnel do not encourage winter travel on the lakes for several reasons. First, they do not have patrols on the lake during winter and staff is minimal. Secondly, there is danger involved from open water or weak ice, avalanches and sudden storms. These hazards mean that, more than any other time of year, the lakes become a wilderness where travellers must be prepared to rely on their own strengths. No one will happen by to bring help.

Dangers and precautions aside, it is a remarkably beautiful trip which average skiers, with better-than-average winter camping skills, can safely make. At present it is infrequently used.

Access and Accommodation
Access is the same as in summer, via Quesnel through Wells to the lakes. The road to Bowron Lake Park is ploughed all winter, but the lodges are closed. Chains should be carried. The only accommodation is in Wells or Quesnel.

Season
The circuit can be travelled between early January and mid-March. The best time is February and early March when the days are a little longer, the cold not so bitter and thaws have sometimes created a good hard crust. Alternatively, thaws may have created slush. Winter temperatures range between 40° and -40°C (104°F to -40°F). Prolonged periods of extreme cold are rare, but possible. Rain may occur at any time of year.

Snow and ice conditions vary greatly from year to year and

day to day. You may experience clear ice or deep snow. Average snowpack in the park is between 62-124 cm (2½-5 feet).

Wildlife

Wildlife you are likely to see in winter includes moose, wolves, river otter, wolverine, fisher, whistling swans, geese, great horned owl, mink, and perhaps caribou. Other small mammals such as squirrels may be seen and a variety of birds.

Route

The suggested route, according to the Parks Branch, is as follows: "Travel the circuit counter-clockwise, starting with Bowron Lake. Break-up is earlier on the west side. Stay on the outside of the circuit on Bowron and Spectacle Lakes. Stay on or close to shore along the Bowron River and Swan Lake. Change to the inside along Skoi Lake, Babcock Lake, Babcock Creek, the Cariboo River, Sandy and Lanezi Lakes. Follow the Upper Cariboo River to McLeary Lake. Stay on shore along the lake and up the Isaac River. The ice on McLeary Lake should be checked carefully, the Cariboo and Isaac Rivers flow through the lake. Change to the outside along Isaac Lake, Indianpoint Lake and Kibbee Lake. The three portage trails between Isaac Lake and the park entrance are easy to travel."

Parties have successfully travelled the circuit in both directions, but those going clockwise may find they are trapped by open water on the west side, necessitating a return or difficult bushwacking.

Safety

The Parks Branch suggests you register with them prior to departure. Because the district office for Bowron is in Williams Lake, registration should be made at Barkerville Historic Townsite. Safety suggestions are:

- Three people should be the minimum party size, four are ideal.
- Travel 3-4 m (10-12 feet) apart, and stay close to shore.
- River ice thickness can change rapidly. Use caution.
- Make a wide circle where streams enter lakes.
- Watch for wet spots, depressions and different colored snow, indicating rotten or weak ice.
- On rivers avoid rocks and other projections since adjacent ice formation will have been retarded by eddies.
- Travel on the inside of curves as the river current has an eroding effect on the outside.

Winter on the Bowron Lakes offers silence and solitude. The trip, however, should be attempted only by those fully experienced in winter camping and well equipped. Weather can vary from sudden storms to a temperature of -40°C (-40°F) and colder.

- At junctions of rivers, turbulence will have slowed ice formation.

- Underground springs are active even at sub-zero temperatures.

- Wide cracks are known to appear on some lakes.

- Travel on clear ice whenever possible.

- Fresh snowfall may hide danger spots. Be extremely careful.

- Do not camp or stop on avalanche chutes along Isaac or Lanezi Lakes.

- If you break through ice, roll on your back and work your way to the edge of solid ice. With your back to the ice, work your elbows up onto the ice and carefully edge the rest of your body onto the solid ice. Crawl backwards until safe.

- If someone else falls in, go to their aid with the help of something to support your weight: skies, branches, rope or ski poles. Have a third person hold the feet of the rescuer and help pull the wet person in.

- Start a fire immediately. Numbness and hypothermia will set in quickly.

Equipment

Obviously, complete equipment for winter camping must be taken. Do not rely on reaching shelters or cabins, both of which may be snowed over. While ski tourers will have their usual gear, the following items are suggested specifically for the lakes or as reminders:

- Repair kit for skis, snowshoes and other equipment.

- Snowshoes: Even for ski parties these are an added safety and convenience item.

- Sleeping bag: Synthetic, in case of water accident and good to well below zero.

- Winter underwear: The new synthetics are ideal.

- Stove, fuel and emergency fire starter.

- Sleds: Some parties find it easier to pull sleds on the lakes rather than carry packs. At times sleds are awkward if bushwacking becomes necessary so a light "crazy carpet" type sled is good. Leave pack straps accessible for bushwacking.

- Shovel, for making camp and avalanche rescue.

- Avalanche cord or beacon.

- First-aid kit.

Because of greatly reduced food availability in winter, for many animals the line between living and dying is fragile. For this reason, travellers should never harass wildlife, especially large mammals such as deer and moose. The extra energy they expend running through deep snow can result in their death.

- Flashlight, lantern, candles, emergency matches.
- Axe, 3/4 size. Spare hatchet.
- Map of circuit, waterproof.
- Fish line and hook for icefishing.
- Sun cream and a peaked or broad-brimmed hat are absolute necessities for sunny weather.
- Camera.
- Animal track field guide.

Note: Axe, shovel, rope and emergency firestarter such as kerosene or diesel fuel should be carried on the outside of your pack, ready for immediate access in case of someone falling through ice.

Chapter Six
The Road to the Lakes

Kilometer 0 (mile 0) Junction
Kilometer zero is the junction of Highway 26 from Quesnel to Barkerville, 1.6 kms (1 mile) from Barkerville. Wells is 72.5 kms (45 miles) from Quesnel. Bowron visitors should plan an extra day to visit the restored gold rush town of Barkerville. For detailed information on the road from Quesnel and the town of Barkerville see *Barkerville*, by Richard Thomas Wright.

km 0.17 (mile 0.1) Williams Creek and the Ballarat Claim
Williams Creek was one of the major gold discoveries of the Cariboo. It is named for "Dutch" Bill Deitz who, with a small party of men, found gold on its headwaters in 1861. The resulting rush drew miners from Antler Creek to Williams Creek where the towns of Richfield, Barkerville, Camerontown and Marysville bloomed and boomed. Gold recovery has totaled over $1,000 per lineal foot on the creek. Gold panning is allowed downstream of this bridge.

The Ballarat Claim lies to the right, or east, of the road, marked by the relocation of the creek and the large piles of dredged gravel. Named for a strike in Australia in 1851, it is one of the oldest continuously worked claims on the creek. It operates under a crown grant from Queen Victoria and has mineral rights to the center of the earth. The claim was recently reworked, in part to recover a gold dredge which sank in the 1950s with the gold unclaimed. Parts of the dredge can still be seen further upstream in the form of the twisted, rectangular pontoons. By the way, trespassing on mineral claims is considered poor manners and sometimes risky. Panning for gold on someone else's claim is downright dangerous.

km 0.24 (mile 0.14) 3100 Road
The 3100, or Cunningham Pass, Road provides access to a network of roads and trails in the Quesnel Highlands. The road is also referred to as the Mathew River Road and, if followed to its termination, reaches the town of Likely on Quesnel Lake. This is a three-hour drive over gravel roads. Watch for logging trucks. The Whiskey Flats Forest Service Campground is just a few miles down this road.

km 0.70 (mile 0.4) Devlin Bench Dredge Ponds

In the 1860s, miners Joseph and Robert Devlin worked this bench on the southeast side of Valley Mountain by running a flume and water from Valley Creek, east of here. Later, the claim was worked with a large dredge which excavated these ponds. More recently, it was successfully reopened and reworked.

km 1.5 (mile 0.9) Weldon Lake Road

A little-travelled track heads to the right. It goes about 1 km (0.6 mile) to Weldon Lake and then wanders along the creek about 2 km (1.2 miles) to French Lake and a junction with the 3100 Road.

km 2.0 (mile 1.2) Moose Ponds

As the road climbs from the Williams Creek Valley, a widening of the road here provides a panoramic view of meadows and pot-hole lakes frequented by moose.

The peak beyond the moose ponds with the missile-like repeater station on top (locals call it "the finger in the sky") is Mount Murray. To the right of Mount Murray is Wendle Mountain and next to it is Mount Greenberry, named for Greenbury Harris, a black man who made charcoal for blacksmiths and boilers. A trail to Murray is described further on.

km 3.0 (mile 1.9) Little Valley Mine

The large meadow that Little Valley Creek runs through was the site of several operations from the time gold was first discovered on Williams Creek. The famous Billy Barker, around whose rich claim the town of Barkerville grew up, sold his interest in the Barker Claim soon after gold was discovered. After he married, and ran out of money, and his wife died, he returned to prospecting. He had a claim here in the 1870s, but was defeated by slum, mud and water that invaded the shaft.

Then in 1902, an English-financed firm under the management of Lester Bonner began the West Canadian Deep Lead Mine, with a shaft that dropped 911 m (278 feet) through bedrock. From the shaft, horizontal drifts reached toward the main channel. The problem was similar to many other mines — too much water. Despite a drainage tunnel, the water continued to flood in. Bonner brought in two boilers, two pumps and 30 Chinese to cut cordwood for the boilers, then later a consulting engineer from England. The mine was only marginally successful. In fact rumor has it that the English backing was Bonner's family trying to keep him in the "Colonies." It closed in 1914 when the outbreak of World War One called many men to service overseas.

Although the various buildings have disappeared, there is

still evidence of the workings on the side hills, and in renewed interest from small placer operations.

km 3.5 (mile 2.1) Yellowhawk Creek Trail to Mount Murray
On the right side of the road is a gravelpit that marks the trailhead of the Yellowhawk Creek trail to Mount Murray. The flagged trail begins on the left side of the pit. After 100 m (300 feet) or so it may be indistinct due to recent clearing and cutting, but it simply climbs over the ridge ahead and can easily be picked up again. An alternative trailhead is a little further along the Bowron Lake Road.

The trail climbs a total of 680 m (2,230 feet) to the repeater station atop Mount Murray, with a return distance of 7 kms (4.3 miles). The trail is easily followed to an old ski cabin, at which point you turn left through a small valley and up alpine meadows to a small tarn and the actual peak. Allow 4-5 hours. The topographical sheet is National Topographic Series, Spectacle Lakes, 93 H/3.

km 4.2 (mile 2.6) Wendle Lake Park
Wendle and Bonner Lakes form a small park suitable for day use. Though large enough for a canoe, it is best suited for some leisurely fishing or a hot afternoon swim. It is the locals' favorite swimming hole. The park is also a delight for anyone interested in wildflowers because Betty Wendle's constant care of the area included planting a number of wild plants. It was through her and Joe's suggestion and work that the area is preserved, thus carries their name. Bonner Lake, a 10-minute walk north, is named for Lester Bonner, as already noted, the manager of the West Canadian Deep Lead Mine, and one of the socialites of early 20th century Barkerville.

km 4.4 (mile 2.7) Mount Murray Winter Trail
A trail to the right goes behind the small roadside ridge and joins the Yellowhawk Creek Trail to Mount Murray. It is popular in winter as it avoids climbing the ridge. Mount Murray has some excellent ski touring for those who don't mind a climb.

km 7.8 (mile 4.8) Jubilee Creek Trail
An alternative to the Yellowhawk Creek Trail, this one takes a different and more difficult route to Mount Murray. It is considered a "thrash" by many locals and is not the preferred route. It is a 9.4-km (5.8-mile) hike, with an elevation gain of 654 m (2,145 feet). Allow between 3-4 hours.

Bowron Lake looking south at Devil's Club Mountain and Sugarloaf.

The Bowron River, below as it leaves the lake, is a rapid-filled trip which should be undertaken only by experienced canoeists.

km 8.7 (mile 5.4) Pines Creek Mining claim

This active mining claim has been in operation for many years. In the years that Bowron was becoming popular it was known as the Nanaimo/Discovery Claim and was owned by John Poole Roddick.

km 9.0 (mile 5.6) Eight Mile Lake - Downie Pass Road

Everyone knew there could be no gold on Eight Mile Creek, but fortunately they didn't tell former Chicago policeman Patrick McKenna and his window-dresser partner, Abe Stott. They went there to fish, and found gold. McKenna died in 1914 at 59 and is buried in the Camerontown Cemetery. Stott died at age 56 and rests in the Stanley Cemetery.

The Eight Mile road goes beyond the lake to Big Valley. At the lake a turn south leads onto the Downie Pass Road, an alternative interesting route to Wells. It is named for Major William Downie, a 39-year-old Scot who came here from California where Downieville is named for him. He made a number of exploring expeditions in the late 1850s, mined around Williams Creek and then went to the Columbia River Big Bend Rush.

km 10.6 to km 12.3 (mile 6.6 to 7.6) Avalanche gates and Cochran viewpoint

A look to the right (east), will quickly explain why this is an avalanche zone and why the mountain above is called Slide Mountain. Keep moving. The gates are for winter road closures when slides occur.

The Mount Cochran viewpoint and sign honors a Bowron pioneer: "James Dean Cochran, 1880-1954. He came to Cariboo in 1912 with his wife Lutie. They settled near the confluence of Bowron River and Indian Point Creek. The rest of their lives were spent trapping, outfitting and surviving. Dean was a man of high principle, honesty, a true naturalist and conservationist."

km 13.0 (mile 8.1) Allan Creek

This creek is likely named for Alexander Allan, editor and owner of Barkerville's *Cariboo Sentinel* newspaper for two years. After he sold out in 1868 he took up mining but was never successful.

km 14.0 (mile 8.7) Devils Creek

km 15.8 (mile 9.8) 1600 Road

This road to the right loops east and south to join up with the 3100 Road. A short distance from this junction are two Forest Service Recreation Sites, Atan Lake and Chisel Lake. The Atan site is a small clearing under conifers with camping and launching for light boats. It is the Takulli Indian word for leaf. It is still marked on some maps as Otter Lake. Chisel Lake is similar, although access to the lake is more difficult and suitable mainly for 4-wheel drive.

A short distance down this road is the site of the old Barkerville Sawmill and Timber Company. At one time there were up to 42 men working here. Much of the lumber for the early restorations at Barkerville, such as the boardwalks and the Wake-Up-Jake, were milled here.

km 17.5 (mile 10.6) 2300/Ketchum Creek Forest Service Road
The 2300 Road heads west along the Willow River to Strathnaver on the Cariboo Highway, between Quesnel and Prince George. A southern branch exits onto Highway 26, Quesnel to Barkerville, at Beaver Pass.

Until 1912 the Barkerville-Bear Lake Road terminated here at Holmshaw's cabin. Barkerville and Bear (Bowron) Lake residents had been lobbying for years to have a road put through the 92 kms (57 miles) to Fraser River via the Wolverine and Goat Rivers. Finally, in 1912 construction began. The *Cariboo Observer* noted on May 23, 1912, that "...a gang of men, in charge of Len Ford, commenced work last Monday on the Barkerville-Fraser River Road. It is the intention of the Government to complete this road as far as Bear lake this season, for which purpose a large number of men will be employed, also several teams of horses with ploughs, graders and scrapers."

The road made it only to the lake. Twenty years later residents were still complaining of the "cross between a trail and a wagon road" which provided access to the lake and still no road to the Fraser. A further history of this road is found under the Goat River Trail.

km 18.5 (mile 11.5) Salina Lake
The property here was pre-empted by W. E. Brown in 1924.

km 18.8 (mile 11.6) Old Road to Left
The descent to Antler Creek here was once called Spratt's Hill. Joe Spratt, an Irishman, worked at several mines in the area and was also hired by Joe Wendle to work on this stretch of road. The route had been surveyed by Seymour Baker to follow the present route. Spratt, however, thought that a route to the west, down a steeper grade, would be more appropriate. There is also a good chance that he was involved in a little placer gold prospecting while the road was being cut and felt his route had better prospects. Because he was "rough and rugged, with a weakness for certain liquid refreshments, which seemed to inspire an aggres-

sive form of sociability," no one was too anxious to argue about his road building.

km 21.0 (mile 13) Antler Creek

In the winter of 1860-61, a small group of prospectors left Keithley Creek on the south side of the Quesnel Highlands and headed upstream, over the Snowshoe Plateau into unprospected areas. From the Highlands they chose one drainage and headed downstream through a pass into a small canyon. There, lying in the sun, exposed in bedrock cracks, lay raw gold — "sun-burn gold" they called it. From one pan they cleared $75, from another, $100. (Gold was then $16 an ounce.) Because there were some deer antlers on the creek's edge they called it Antler Creek. Their discovery triggered the Cariboo gold rush which a decade later resulted in the birth of the Province of British Columbia.

The site of Antler Creek was a few miles upstream from this point, but prospectors soon floated downstream on a variety of craft not only to prospect but also to try to reach the Bear River (now Bowron) and the Fraser.

km 22.6 (mile 14) Bowron Lake Park Boundary

Boundary of the 121,600-ha (300,352-acre) provincial park.

km 24.2 (mile 15) West Side Road

This side road goes to the government wharf used by cottagers on the west side and the Parks Branch compound.

km 24.4 (mile 15.2) Becker's Lodge

Becker's Lodge, formerly the Cariboo Hunting and Fishing Lodge, was built in 1933 by Grover Youngs. Now operated by Lothar Vollmar, it offers accommodation, a good restaurant, camping, showers, canoe rentals and limited supplies.

km 24.7 (mile 15.3) Bowron Lake

Formerly known as Bear Lake, this lake was named for John Bowron, an Overlander of '62, who came to the Cariboo in search of gold. He became one of the leading civil servants and administrators of the Williams Creek area. This launching point is for those paddling the west side.

Bowron Lake Lodge and Resorts hold the lakefront property here. The land was pre-empted by Joe Wendle in 1909 and purchased by Bill McKitrick in 1935. Now the third generation of McKitricks operate the lodge. Accommodation, restaurant, camping, showers and canoe rentals are available. The lodge and its history are further described in the People of the Lakes section.

km 25.3 (Mile 15.7) Bowron River Bridge
This is the outlet of Bowron Lake, and for skilled paddlers the beginning of a 174-km (108-mile) canoe trip down the Bowron River to the Fraser, described elsewhere in this book.

km 25.5 (mile 15.8) Bear River Mercantile
Sandy and Dick Phillips moved here several years ago to begin this operation. It is situated on the site of the former Boisie Lodge, owned by Jack Boise. George Turner's house was located just to the north of the present store.

km 25.6 (mile 15.9) Bowron River Road
The road to the left goes along the northeast side of the Bowron River for several miles, providing access to logging sites and several homes and ranches. The road links several logging operations and eventually reaches Highway 16 near Purden Lake, east of Prince George. In the early days of Bowron country development, several families had farms or homes down this road.

A short distance down the road was the homestead of Albert Littlefield who pre-empted here in 1909, next door to Frank Kibbee. In the 1920s, Littlefield was the public works road foreman in this district, with trapping and farming as a sideline, and lived here at the lake. In the winter of 1923, he went to Seattle for a holiday and suffered a major illness. He died there on February 5. Littlefield Creek which flows into Kruger Creek is named for him.

km 25.7 (mile 16) Kibbee's Cabin
The property on the lake front is the site of Frank Kibbee's east side cabin.

km 26.6 (mile 16.5) Bowron Lake Registration Centre
The road ends at the campground, parking lot and registration centre.

The campground has 25 campsites, including 3 doubles, with room for recreational vehicles. There are no hookups. Remember, all canoeists must register. For more park information see Preparing For The Chain.

Chapter Seven
The Bowron Chain

The complete circuit of the lakes is a total of 116 kms (72 miles) with 6 portages totalling 8-9.6 kms (5-6 miles), if Isaac River cannot be run. Camping is allowed only at designated sites. As many of these sites are small and suitable only for a single party, it is advisable to camp early. The sites with shelters are larger but in periods of inclement weather become crowded. Groups are confined to camping at group sites. Similarly, the sites with cabins are popular, again particularly after a long wet spell. Remember: check your gear carefully and take extra food.

Directions, left and right, indicate the side of the circuit when travelling in the normal clockwise direction around the circuit. Except in Babcock Creek, river right is always the right side when facing downstream.

km 0 (mile 0) Registration Centre. Portage to Kibbee Lake - 2.4 kms (1.5 miles)

All canoeists using the chain must register. Winter travellers should register in Barkerville.

Your departure may be delayed here to ensure that parties are spaced on the lakes. Do not be tempted to rush to Isaac Lake the first day. Spend some time on Kibbee and Indianpoint Lakes.

The Bowron Lake journey begins with this 2.4-km (1.5-mile) portage to Kibbee Lake. The first half of the trail is a gradual uphill climb. The trail levels at the halfway point and, just before the lake, descends gradually. If you think this is a long carry be glad that you weren't here before the 1960s when the portage followed the old Goat River Trail and bypassed Kibbee Lake, meaning a 8-km (5-mile) carry to begin the circuit. Since then the trail has been relocated and upgraded.

In 1983-84 most of the portage trails were rebuilt with new boardwalks replacing rotting, ankle-twisting corduroy. But since then the hard-to-maintain and often slippery boardwalks have been torn up in favor of solid earthen trails. One way to ease the strain is to carry your canoe and some gear in to Kibbee Lake the night before you begin, camping at the Bowron Lake site. If you do so remember to use the cache for any gear left at Kibbee.

Midway along the trail is a sign describing the 1975 blow-down, and warning of fire danger:

"Blowdown. 100-130 km/h (60-80 mile-an-hour) winds hit

A canoe party's gear stacked on a bluff overlooking Bowron Lake, ready for a 12-day paddle around the chain.

Small and peaceful Kibbee Lake, below, is the start of the 116-km (72-mile) wilderness experience.

these trees on Nov. 15, 1975. 1,000 acres of forest fell. Nature's reforestation crew is hard at work. Young spruce are replacing old lodgepole pines. "Fire danger is extreme. Please - no matches, cigarettes or fires for 1.2 km (3/4 mile). Next campground is at the east end of Kibbee Lake 5 km (3.1 miles) by trail and canoe. Thank you for co-operating. Parks supervisor."

The Bowron Lake circuit has a great variety of plantlife, only a small portion of which has been recorded. This trail to Kibbee Lake has as wide a variety of plants as anywhere in the park. While resting at the canoe props, have a look around for some of the following plants: lady fern, baneberry, trefoil foamflower, swamp gooseberry, sylvan goatsbeard, large-leaved avens, red raspberry, thimbleberry, trailing rubus, Sitka mountain-ash, yellow wood violet, alpine willow-herb, fireweed, sarsaparilla, cow-parsnip, bunchberry, Labrador tea, large wintergreen, northern starflower, marsh skullcap, Indian paintbrush, western twinflower, mountain red elder, Sitka valerian, pearly everlasting, broad-leaf arnica, Lindley aster, arrowleaf groundsel, cotton-grass, Queen's cup, false Solomon's seal and ladies' tresses.

Where the lake drains into Kibbee Creek there is a striking widespread bloom in mid-July of the tall white bog-orchid. This orchid's common names are clues to its appearance: tall white bog-orchid, leafy white orchid, bog-candle and scent-candle. It is 3-6 m (1-2 feet) in height with bright green leaves and a dense spike of waxy white flowers. The radish-like tubers of this plant were gathered and eaten by native people but it is now considered too rare to use for food. Remember, no plants may be picked in the park.

km 2.4 (mile 1.5) Kibbee Lake - 2.4 kms (1.5 miles) long
Where Kibbee Lake drains out through Kibbee Creek over a beaverdam the canoe is put in the water for the first time. Kibbee Lake is named for Frank Kibbee, a trapper and guide in the area for many years. Kibbee Lake and Creek, which the portage trail follows was, like several other creeks and lakes, called Beaver Lake until the early 1900s.

Halfway down the lake on the left side there is a small cabin, built by one of the area's guides. A few yards away is a long beaver dam across a creek that drains Thompson Lake, a small lake on the north side of Kibbee Lake. It is accessible from the beaver dam.

Campsite #1, a group site, is located at the end of the this first portage. Campsite #2, a large site with six to eight pads, is at the east end of Kibbee Lake at the beginning of the next portage.

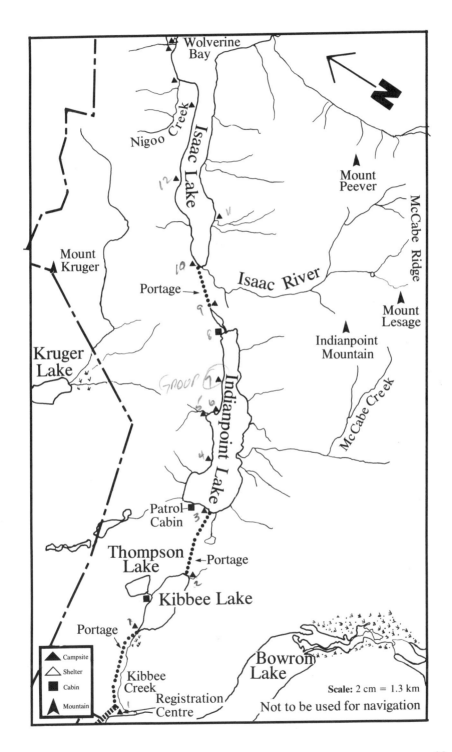

Wolverine
Bay

Nigoo Creek

Isaac Lake

Mount
Peever

McCabe Ridge

Mount
Kruger

Portage →

Isaac River

Mount
Lesage

Kruger
Lake

Indianpoint
Mountain

Indianpoint Lake

McCabe Creek

Patrol
Cabin

Thompson
Lake

← Portage

Kibbee Lake

Bowron
Lake

Portage

Kibbee
Creek

Registration
Centre

Scale: 2 cm = 1.3 km
Not to be used for navigation

Campsite
Shelter
Cabin
Mountain

83

km 3.6 (mile 2.2) Thompson Lake

This small lake sits like a blister on the north side of Kibbee Lake. The lake is named after the Thompson brothers (see the People of the Lakes section) who began a small homestead on the lake in 1916. On topographic sheets it is marked as Lot 9547. Their trapline ran north toward Kruger Lake.

km 4.8 (mile 3) Indianpoint Lake Portage - 2.0 kms (1.2 miles) long

This portage has three canoe rests to break the long carry. There is a good campsite at the Indianpoint end with leveled, gravelled tentsites looking out onto Indianpoint Lake. For those not wanting to reload their canoe and paddle further, this is a good first night's camp. One person can begin setting up camp while another returns for gear. Gear cached in this area should have all zippers covered or locked. Trinket and food-stealing ravens have adapted to the zipper revolution with new skills and can easily unzip packs in lakeshore robbery.

km 6.8 (mile 4) Indianpoint Lake - 6.4 kms (3.8 miles) long

A little north along the lake shore is a Parks Branch Ranger cabin. These patrol cabins are usually manned by Parks Branch staff who have first-aid skills and emergency radio communications. Any power boats seen on lakes other than Bowron Lake will be operated by park's staff.

Campsite #3, a large site, is at the end of the portage. A 1912 map of the Goat River Trail indicates that someone named Develt had a cabin at the outlet of Indianpoint Creek.

Until recently, the lake and the mountain above were written as two words, Indian Point. The origin of the name is lost but it was named as early as 1869, and likely relates to the Bear Lake tribe.

This was once the home of Thomas and Eleanor McCabe. Across the lake, McCabe Creek flows in from McCabe Ridge and, high above the stone chimney of their old home, an eagle's eyrie plays lonely sentinel to what was once a beautiful home in the wilderness. (The McCabe's story is told in the People of the Lakes section.)

The foundations that remain since the Parks Branch burned the house can be found on a small rise above Indianpoint Creek on the north side of the lake, marked by the chimney which can be seen from the patrol cabin. Wandering through the ruins, one can imagine what it must have been like to live here several decades ago. It is harder to imagine them actually having built a corduroy road for their car. Sections of the road can still be found.

Canoeists should watch for a wind that often blows out of McCabe Creek.

km 9.6 (mile 6) Kruger Bay Campsite

This small bay on the left of Indianpoint Lake is surrounded by several pleasant campsites: #4 and 5, medium sites with 3-5 pads; #6, a large site, and group site #7. Being at the end of two portages and a short paddle, they often mark the end of the trippers' first day and are frequently filled with recuperating canoeists.

km 12.2 (mile 7.6) Indianpoint Cabin

At the Indianpoint Lake narrows is a small cabin built by Frank Cushman as part of his Wolverine Mountain guiding operation. There is a small campsite here, #8. The canoe route wanders through a small marsh, marked by colored poles, as the lake narrows towards the next portage.

km 13.2 (mile 8.2) Indianpoint Lake Campsite #9 and Portage - 1.6 kms (1 mile) long

Located at the beginning of the portage trail, this site has little to recommend it, except the trail end. It is a sheltered, shady site, rocky and with few level areas. Use the bear cache when you portage.

This portage trail has a climb and descent which, though slight, makes it a little more difficult. It is shorter than the last portages, with two canoe rests. This was once part of a 98-ha (40-acre) parcel pre-empted by Joe Wendle in 1928.

km 14.8 (mile 9.2) Isaac Lake - 38 kms (23.6 miles) long

Isaac Lake (elevation 948 m, (3,109 feet) was not discovered until a few years after the Cariboo gold rush had enticed miners and prospectors to the Quesnel Highlands and Cariboo Mountains area. It was generally referred to as Big Lake in the early years. Frederick Daly, a Barkerville photographer, wrote in 1869 about the area between Barkerville and Tete Jaune Cache:

"...and the region between is a sea of mountains and densely wooded with several large lakes and one of the latter recently discovered a few miles from Bear Lake (Bowron) is said to be 60 miles in length."

Although Daly was out by over half, Isaac is indeed a large lake with the west arm to Wolverine Bay being 6.8 kms (4.2 miles) and the main arm, 31.2 kms (19.4 miles). Particularly on the main arm, storms can rise quickly, sweeping down the lake in brief minutes. Canoeists should stay close to shore, prepared to land should a squall rise. The usual route, and the safest, is on the left, or outside of the lake, where camping areas are located.

Campsite #10 is at the end of the portage, a small site. There

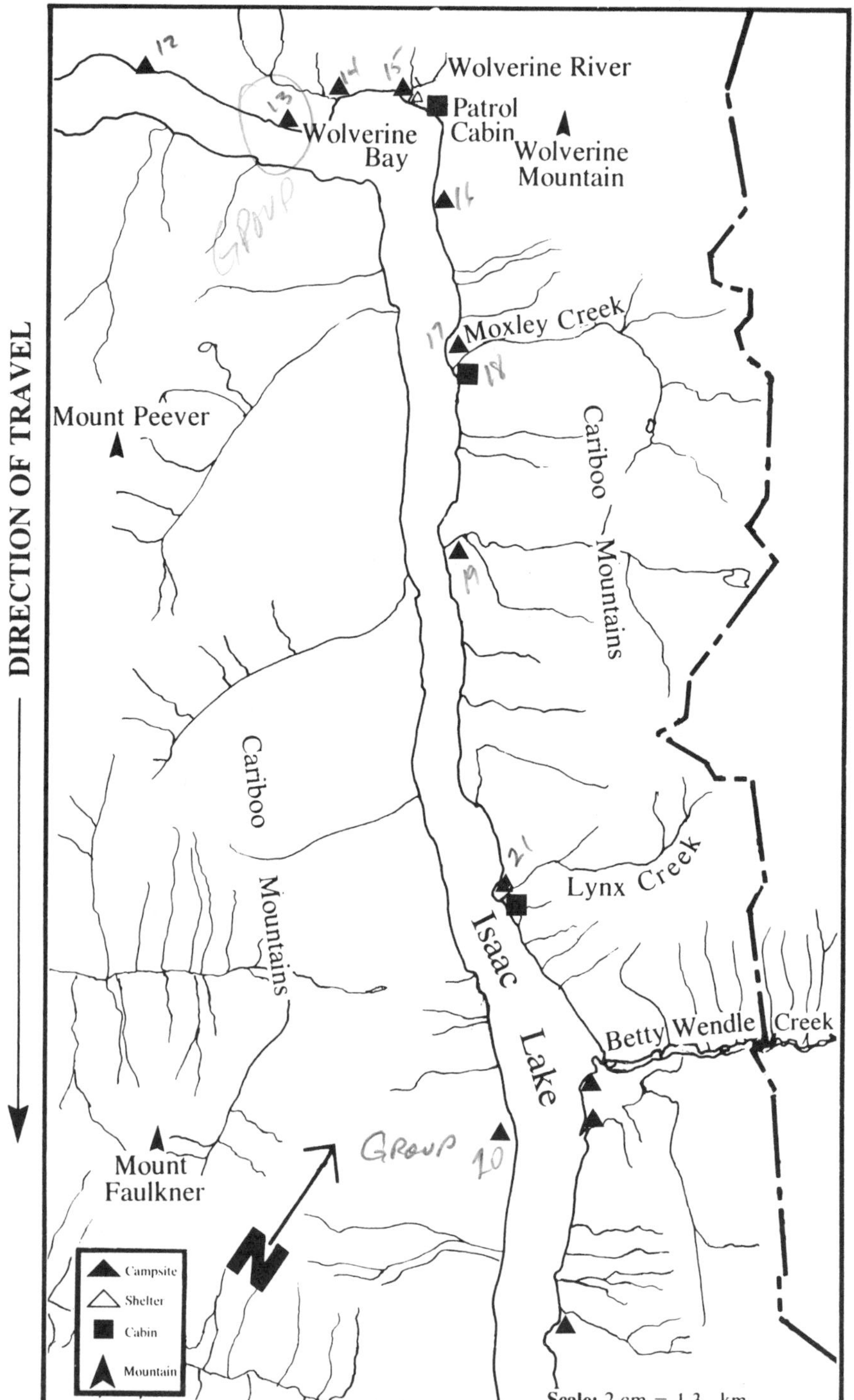

DIRECTION OF TRAVEL

Wolverine River

Patrol Cabin

Wolverine Bay

Wolverine Mountain

Mount Peever

Moxley Creek

Cariboo Mountains

Cariboo Mountains

Lynx Creek

Isaac Lake

Betty Wendle Creek

Mount Faulkner

GROUP 20

N

▲	Campsite
△	Shelter
■	Cabin
▲	Mountain

Scale: 2 cm = 1.3 km

Not to be used for navigation

are two small campsites, #11 and 12; a medium site, #14; and one group site, #13 on the left, or outside of the circuit, before Wolverine Bay. One new site, #12, is located on the right side about 2 kms (1.2 miles) along the lake.

km 20.6 (mile 12.8) Nigoo Creek Campsite
Nigoo Creek flows into Wolverine from behind a ridge on the west. There is a group campsite here, #13. Formerly called Beaver Creek, Nigoo is Takulli for teeth.

km 21.6 (mile 13.4) Cabins, Shelter, Campsite
Here are a Ranger cabin, a backcountry cabin, a shelter and a large campsite, #15, where several trappers had their cabins. The Brierley Bros. had a cabin here in 1912 and later Ole Nelson, a Swedish trapper, had his base camp at the Wolverine's mouth. Nelson came from Sweden in 1922 and arrived in the Barkerville area during the 1930s depression gold rush. He brought Eric Woltertin's trapline in the Goat River Valley and worked it, with periodic seasons as a miner, until 1965. In 1930 W. Barrett preempted 38 ha (95 acres) at the creek mouth.

Wolverine Bay is famous for its large lake trout. Nelson evidently caught one weighing almost 9 kgs (19 pounds).

Across the lake to the south is Mount Peever, named for Flying Officer Rolland N. Peever, Royal Canadian Air Force, a resident of Wells who was killed in action in 1944.

Directly above the bay is Wolverine Mountain, 2,056 m (6,743 feet), a peak that can be climbed by those vigourous enough to scramble up the avalanche slide that skids into the lake. Should you decide to climb, beware of bears. Make lots of noise and keep your eyes open.

Across the lake on the main arm is another blowdown similar to the one on the Kibbee Lake portage. On the left side of the main arm, above the Moxley Creek cabin, is an old burn. Dead and red conifers mark the work of pine bark beetles, an infestation that has reached epidemic proportions in recent years.

For several years logging companies have used the dying conifers as reasoning that areas of the park should be logged to stop the spread. So far they have been held off at the park boundary, but each year the roar of chainsaws and trucks comes closer. In the winter of 1984 loggers reached areas on the north side of the park. Scars of a large clearcut can now be seen from Wolverine Bay. The park boundary is only a mile east.

This Wolverine Valley is the site of the Goat River Trail, and would be the route of a highway being proposed, linking this area with the Robson Valley along the Fraser River (see Goat River Trail).

The long arm of Isaac Lake can appear formidable to novice paddlers. Apparent progress is lost on the long expanse. One way to alleviate this somewhat disheartening situation is to stay close to shore, where progress is more noticeable, and to paddle from point to point or campsite to campsite. After one long, trying, wind-swept day a paddler was heard to remark: "Paddle point to point! I was just trying for tree to tree."

It is 31.2 kms (19.4 miles) to the campsite and shelter at the southern end of Isaac Lake, with 10 campsites and one group site on the way. The first is campsite #16, a medium-size site a short distance down the left side.

km 25.7 (mile 16) Moxley Creek Cabin and Campsites #17-18
The creek is named for J. Wells Moxley, a trapper in the area from 1897 to 1901. Earlier it was called Moose Creek. Most of the cabins on the circuit, such as this one, site 18, are small and over 50 years old. In the early 1990s all were reroofed and foundations rebuilt. The cabins are meant as emergency accommodations. Should another party arrive, it is customary and good manners to share the cabin, wood and stove.

Campsite #19, a medium-size site, is at the mouth of an unnamed creek between here and Lynx Creek.

km 33.3 (mile 20.7) Lynx Creek Campsite #21 and Cabin
The large clearing at the mouth of Lynx Creek is not only the result of creek erosion but also the construction of a helicopter landing pad, built in an emergency several years ago. A family was camping here and on a still, breezeless day the heavy limb of a cottonwood fell on the tent where a woman was changing, pinning and severely injuring her.

A team of canoeists set out to get help from the nearest patrol cabin at Wolverine Bay. They, in turn, radioed headquarters staff who dispatched a helicopter and ordered the construction of this pad. The clearing and pad were built by two park's employees in a little over an hour, just as the helicopter swooped over the lake. The woman was flown to Williams Lake, arriving at sunset, with the pilot landing by the aid of street lights. The heli-pad is a primitive memorial to the rescue team whose fast work saved the canoeist's life.

Canoeists are advised to keep in mind which direction leads to the closest patrol cabin in case of emergency. Do not camp or put gear near the landing pads.

The Lynx cabin is comfortable. The campsite, #21, is large. A game trail runs a short distance south along the lake shore.

Isaac Lake looking south from Wolverine Bay.

On Isaac River portages are necessary since the waterway includes an 11-m- (36-foot-) high waterfall.

Across Isaac Lake is Ford Peak, another mountain named for a serviceman, Corporal Reginald C. Ford of Wells, killed in action November 1944.

Along the west side of the lake the forest cover is almost entirely Western hemlock. On the east side it is mixed with Western red cedar. The large-leaved deciduous trees generally found along the lake shores or at creek mouths are black cottonwood. Mixed with them are occasional birch, which in autumn turns the woods a bright yellow.

km 36.5 (mile 22.7) Betty Wendle Creek and Campsite #21a
Betty Wendle Creek flows into Isaac Lake from the east. The creek is named for Joe Wendle's wife. At one time they had a cabin on the creek's delta. There is often a wind coming out of the valley onto Isaac Lake. On the broad alluvial fan is a small campsite, and immediately across the lake a group site.

This valley is one area that many would like to see included in Bowron Lake Provincial Park. The boundary now is only some 3 km (2 miles) away and, should logging reach into the Betty Wendle Creek Valley, it would be seen and heard from Isaac Lake.

The valley across the lake is the headwaters of Huckey Creek, a tributary of the Bowron River. On the left is Mount Faulkner, the eastern end of Tediko Ridge and, on the right, Ford Peak at the end of McLeod Ridge. Mount Faulkner is named in memory of another soldier, Gunner Thomas L. Faulkner of Wells, killed in action in September 1944.

Tediko Ridge is the Takulli word for "girls." How it relates to the ridge is anyone's guess. McLeod Ridge, on the other hand, is named for Kenneth McLeod, the trapper partner of the "Swamp Angel" whose story is told elsewhere.

This is a large campsite. It is 16.3 km (10 miles) to the campsites and shelter at the southern end of Isaac Lake, with five small campsites along the way. Group site #20 is across the lake.

km 41.7 (mile 25.9) Isaac Lake Campsite #22
Directly across the lake from this campsite can be seen the headwaters of the Bowron River. It begins only 150 m (500 feet) above the lake and about 2 kms (just over 1 mile) west.

Campsite #22 is a small one. Campsites #23, medium; #24, small; and #25, medium, are between here and Bowron Creek.

km 48 (mile 30) Bowman Creek Campsite #26
Amos Bowman is known to any Cariboo historian because he drew some of the most detailed goldfields maps that exist. Accurate even today, they show buildings, shafts, geological fea-

tures and survey lines. This creek and Mount Amos Bowman are named for him. The cirques that face the lake here, and the hollows at the heads of the glacial valleys below the peaks, are examples of the glacial formations in the Cariboo Mountains. On the opposite side of the lake, several of the creeks that drop out of the Mowdish Range cascade into the lake as waterfalls.

There is a small campsite here and another medium site, #27, just before the end of the lake.

km 52.8 (mile 32.8) Campsites #28 and 29, and McLeary Lake Portage - 2.8 kms (1.7 miles) long

Like Wolverine Bay, this is another large campsite with several pads, a log shelter with stove and sheltering trees. There is also a group site. This is a popular site because it is at the head of the portage trail and the river chute, and at the end of the long paddle down Isaac Lake. It is frequently crowded with wet paddlers.

Rumor has it the Hudson's Bay Company had a post or cache here in the 1800s. Although it is not mentioned in HBC records, it may have been a simple cabin where a post trader met Takullis to trade for furs or fish, or a camp for HBC Iroquois trappers. Usually the natives would have travelled down the Bowron and Fraser Rivers to Fort George.

Experienced canoeists can run the chute and/or the top part of the Isaac River, cutting off about 1.6 kms (1 mile) of walking. The safer alternative is to carry across the point the camp is on, bypassing the chute and entering the river in a backeddy. Canoe downstream a short distance and watch on the left for your takeout. Then cache your equipment and head south. If running the chute, be sure you are wearing your PFD. A portage trail bypasses this whole section of river if you are unsure of moving water strokes.

The original trail, still marked on many maps, continued down the left side of the river to McLeary Lake. While this trail still exists as a rough slash, it is now expected that canoeists will launch into the river again below the Isaac River Cascades.

Canoe a short distance, crossing to the right side above a log jam and 11-m- (36-foot-) high Isaac Falls. Take out and carry south to McLeary Lake. On this last short portage there are several side trails to the left that will take you to the river side for a view of the falls, well worth the short hike.

km 55.6 (mile 34.5) McLeary Lake, Campsite #30, and Becker's Cabin #31

The McLeary Lake campsite, a medium-size site, is around the corner, across the lake. It is an open site with a panoramic view

DIRECTION OF TRAVEL

Mount Foreman

Turner Creek

Isaac Lake

Mount Amos Bowman

Bowman Creek

Lanezi Lake

Experienced canoeists only

Portage

Cascades (unnavigable)

Trail

Logjam

Portage

Falls 12m

Cariboo River

Patrol Cabin

Iron Slough

Kilakuai Creek

Campsite
Shelter
Cabin
Mountain

Scale: 2 cm = 1.3 km
Not to be used for navigation

of McLeary Lake and the surrounding mountains. This site offers an evening paddle of McLeary and a walk along the old east bank portage trail to view Isaac Falls.

On the lake's far side, near a slough, is a cabin sometimes used as a patrol cabin, so don't count on it being available. Trapper Fred Becker's base camp trap cabin was near here. He had another on his trap line up the Cariboo River (then called the Upper Swamp River) in Hanging Valley.

McLeary Lake is named for a forgotten trapper. It is not difficult, if you are here on a winter day, to imagine a lonely man and his dog striding across the lake's surface. With "misery slippers" (snowshoes) dangling, he swings his feet wide in a bear-like gait, a long pole in one hand in case he should hit weak ice. On his back is a pack of traps and fresh furs and over a shoulder a rifle. Behind, the tracks are swept away before the wind and the lone figure vanishes in a crystal mist of frost. It is a scene that was once a common sight on these lakes since it was the trappers who travelled here for decades before recreationists.

The water of McLeary Lake is affected by the rise and fall of the Cariboo River. It is a backwater formed by the confluence of the two rivers. For this reason it is not safe to simply pull your canoe up and leave it. Rising water may drift it away. Always tie up.

Winter travellers may have trouble in this area. If McLeary Lake's ice cannot be crossed due to the heavy flow of water, you will have to continue up the portage trail on river right — as noted, right and left are always figured when looking downstream — and cross the river above the falls. If this route is not possible, you will have to bushwack up the right side of the river.

km 56.8 (mile 35.3) Cariboo River

The Cariboo River is the site of most canoeing accidents, swampings and spills on the circuit. The river is constantly changing in response to high or low flows, fallen trees and silting. Depending on the time of year and weather conditions, the water of the Cariboo River can fluctuate five fold. In low water it may be difficult to float over wide riffles and around snags and small log jams. In high water these hazards will disappear but the heavier flow will demand caution on curves and near sweepers.

Before attempting this trip, you should have learned a few basic strokes and safety procedures such as self-rescue. This is not the time for a lesson, so use caution and stay well away from any obstacle, including stumps, sweepers and the outside of bends. If need be, get out and line around a hazard. Help is a long way off and the least you risk in a capsize is losing equipment and getting a soaking. A speed slower than the current will allow maneuvering, therefore backpaddling is a common whitewater stroke. Backpaddling slows the canoe and allows time for quick direction changes.

km 60.4 (mile 37.5) Iron Slough

The large slough to the south of the Cariboo River is fed by Kilakuai Creek, formerly Grizzly Creek. Kilakuai is, by one account, the Takulli term for iron; by another, the word for nails. Maybe rusty nails, for the inference is to the reddish colored water in the slough.

The mountain to the south, unnamed on maps, is known as "The Jellymold" to locals because of its distinctive shape.

There is a small campsite, #32, on river left near the mouth of this creek.

km 62 (mile 38.5) Lanezi Lake - 14.8 kms (9.2 miles) long

Lanezi, elevation 908 m 2,978 feet, is a long, narrow lake bordered on the north by Needle Point Ridge, including Kaza and Bryan Peaks, and on the south by the mountains surrounding Ishpa Mountain. Kaza is the Takulli word for arrow. Bryan Peak is named in memory of Sergeant Guy N. Bryan, Royal Canadian Air Force, of Wells, killed in action November 1941.

There are five campsites, one at either end, and three along the north shore, with one group site near Turner Creek. The largest is Turner Creek, 4 kms (2.5 miles) along the north side. All Lanezi sites are on the north shore. Since landing sites are few, it is recommended that paddlers travel the north shore in case a wind rises.

Lanezi was named Mountain Lake in 1869 by explorer Fred Black, and then Long Lake until 1932. Lanezi, according to the Geographical Branch, is the Takulli word for ten, perhaps suggesting its length is close to 16 kms (10 miles).

The first campsite is #32a, a small site just west of the river mouth on the north side.

km 66.4 (mile 41) Turner Creek and Campsite #34

Turner Creek is named for George Turner, a Bowron Lake settler and game warden (see People of the Lakes section).

There is a medium-size tent site and a shelter west of the creek mouth. Group site #33 is slightly to the east. The shelter has been closed in and a stove added to make drying more effective for those who upset in the Cariboo River.

The next two small sites on Lanezi, #35 and 36, are on the

94

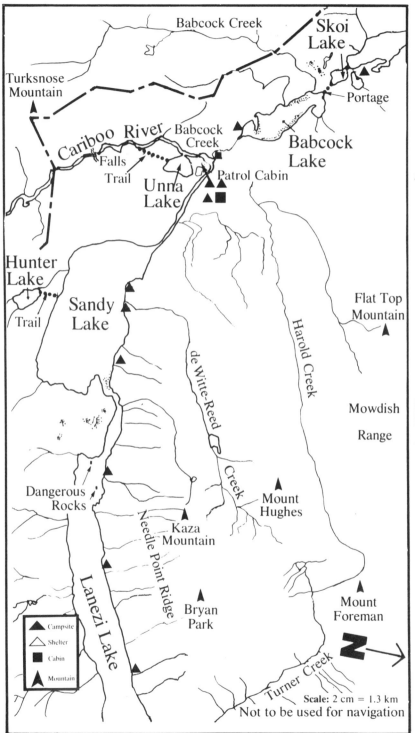

Babcock Creek

Skoi Lake

Turksnose Mountain

Portage

Cariboo River
Babcock Creek

Babcock Lake

Falls
Trail

Patrol Cabin

Unna Lake

Hunter Lake

Trail

Sandy Lake

Flat Top Mountain

Harold Creek

de Witte-Reed

Creek

Mowdish

Range

Dangerous Rocks

Mount Hughes

Zeedle Point Ridge

Kaza Mountain

Lanezi Lake

Bryan Park

Mount Foreman

N

Turner Creek

▲ Campsite
△ Shelter
■ Cabin
▲ Mountain

Scale: 2 cm = 1.3 km
Not to be used for navigation

DIRECTION OF TRAVEL

95

north side. They are both small sites. A third is at the lake outfall.

km 74.0 (mile 46) Morris-Reed Point
On the right side of the lake a rocky headland juts out. One face has a shelf, a good place to sit and sun. In 1926 two men painstakingly chipped into the rock:

OHIO
MORRIS-REED
1926.

The carvers were Floyd de Witte Reed, (see km 81.2 (mile 50.4) and his friend, Morris, Ohions who came to the Cariboo as young men to trap and hunt. Floyd, known as "Big Reed," was a sometimes partner of Frank Kibbee (see People of the Lakes).

In the spring of 1926, Reed was fishing on Long Lake (Lanezi) and put out a line while cooking supper. He baited the hook with a minnow. On his return less than half an hour later he found that a 6-inch fish had swallowed the minnow. An 18-inch fish had swallowed the 6-inch and a 36-inch had swallowed the 18-inch. Then a 5-foot fish swallowed the 3-foot fish, and that a much larger fish had arrived and was viewing the bait from various angles. Reed figured the line had reached its limit and pulled it in. (A fishy story? And not even in metric!)

Reed said Isaac Lake had Long Lake skinned a mile for fish and that only minnows got down to Long Lake.

Across the lake from Morris-Reed Point are the rocky peaks of Ishpa Mountain. Once named The Pyramid for its shape, the mountain has since been named for the Takulli word meaning My Father.

Watch for two rock outcroppings in the lake beyond here, one on the right shore and another on the left.

km 76.8 (mile 47.7) Cariboo River - 1.2 kms (.75 mile) long and Campsite #37
There is a medium campsite at the lake's outfall, on the right.

More of a narrow lake than a river, this short section of river has no noticeable elevation drop and is easily canoed. At the west end of the channel stay left or you will be grounded on sand bars that reach out from the right shore.

km 78.0 (mile 48) Soda Spring Salt Licks
On the left shore as you enter Sandy Lake is an area that Fred Becker used to call Soda Springs. It is a good place to watch for animals coming to the mineral deposits.

km 78.8 (mile 48.9) Sandy Lake - 4.8 kms (3 miles) long
Sandy Lake often offers canoeists a respite from rain and drizzle.

96

Sandy Lake, a name which reflects its beautiful sandy beaches.

It is a large flat pan filled with water shallow enough that it is often warm. The campsite at km 81.2 (mile 50.4) sits on the lake's sunny side, fronted by sandy beaches. As evidenced by the changing vegetation, this is usually a drier area than the Isaac side, a good place for a lay-over day.

The warmer water often means that in winter the ends of the lake are open, so skiers will have to cautiously skirt open water. Whistling swans winter here, feeding where warm springs keep the water open. It is a spectacular area in winter's coat. The swans are likely the reason explorer Frank Black named it Swan Lake in 1869. Later, the north end of Spectacle became known as Swan Lake.

Group campsite #37a is on the right, just beyond the river mouth.

km 81.2 (mile 50.4) de Witte Reed Creek and Campsites #38 - 39
With warm southern exposures and sandy beaches, these two large sites at the creek mouth are prime both winter and summer. The creek is named for Floyd de Witte Reed.

Across the lake is a short trail, about 1 km (.6 mile), leading to Hunter Lake, once a reasonably good fly-fishing lake. It offers a welcome change from sitting in a canoe. Unfortunately, logging roads from the Mathew River allowed easy access and it

Because the Cariboo River below McLeary Lake fluctuates so much, at times canoes have to be carried over sandbars.

was fished out. Camping and campfires are not permitted at Hunter Lake.

km 82.8 (mile 51) Cariboo River - 3.6 kms (2.2 miles) long

The Cariboo River from Sandy Lake to Babcock Creek is easily canoed by novices. It flows slowly and allows plenty of room and time for maneuvering. Those wishing to camp at the little gems of Unna and Rum Lakes should proceed 400 m (1,300 feet) past Babcock Creek and watch for the narrow opening to Unna Lake on the left.

Do not proceed down the Cariboo River past Unna Lake. Cariboo Falls is just downstream.

km 86.2 (mile 53.5) Harold Creek

Harold Creek flows in on the right side. It is named after Harold Mason who lived in the area from 1910 to 1929 (see People of the Lakes). In the past it was known as Mason Creek, but was changed to the more familiar Harold.

km 86.8 (mile 53.9) Unna Lake Campsites #40-42

There may be a temptation to turn right at Babcock Creek and continue on without detouring, but Unna, formerly Grizzly Lake, is such a beauty that it is well worth stopping for at least a day or two. The lake mirrors the surrounding mountains and

98

its open vegetation provides good camping area. Those seeking solitude can sneak through the reeds at the north end and enter Rum Lake, now a campsite area. Rum Lake is actually only about a 98-m (300-foot) walk from the shores of the Cariboo River above Babcock Creek. Evidence of old camps can be found here, including an old fish smokehouse.

Unna Lake is a kettle hole in the large glacial outwash plain of the Cariboo River. The vegetation in this area is quite different from other parts of the park. It is a rain-shadow area, thus much drier. Instead of fir, hemlock or cedar, the dominant trees are lodgepole pine. Where usually the forest floor has been covered with an almost impenetrable growth of devil's club, willow and other ground cover, it is now open with scattered clumps of dwarf juniper.

Saskatoon, or serviceberry, can be found and in some areas false box forms a ground cover, though this latter plant has become increasingly rare during the last century due to moose browsing. A similar ground cover found here is kinnikinnick, or bear berry, a low growing, trailing plant with thick leathery evergreen leaves up to one inch long. The leaves of this plant were often used by Takullis and early travellers as a tobacco substitute or extender. Its small, bright red berries were eaten or crushed and used as a lotion.

Particularly along the Cariboo Falls trail, snowberry (not to be confused with waxberry) creeps over logs in extensive mats. It is recognized by thick leaves up to 6 mm (1/4 inch) long, with hairs on stem leaves and fruit.

One-sided winter green is found along the trail, along with Canada blueberry, pipsissewa, spreading dogbane, and western twinflower. If you are fortunate you will find a few clumps of the tiny beautiful Calypso orchid, *Calypso bulbosa*.

In these dry areas a bright red berry with rusty spots on the leaves can be found. It is called soopolallaie, or soap berry. While edible, it is easily identified by its bitter flavor and strong after-taste. The berry is used to make "Skahoosum," or Takulli ice cream. A couple of tablespoons of berries are whipped into a froth, sweetened with wild strawberries or sugar, and beaten to a meringue-like consistency. The bitter taste may not suit palates accustomed to an overabundance of sugar, but with added sweets it makes a good outdoor treat.

From the south end of Cariboo Falls there is an easy 1.5-km (1-mile) trail through open lodgepole pine forest to Cariboo Falls, 26 m (85 feet) high. The best view is by walking as far as possible on the trail and looking back. To the southeast near the falls are two lakes which locals have tagged Rete and Jean Lakes.

Several Barkerville-Wells residents had cabins on Rum and

Unna Lakes in the years before it was made a park. One of them still stands on the point of land dividing the lake from the Cariboo River. Another has been moved to the patrol cabin compound for use as storage.

There is a group campsite, #41, and a small site, #42, on Rum Lake. At Unna there is an excellent large campsite, #40, and a cabin.

To continue on the circuit, leave Unna Lake and paddle upstream 400 m (1,300 feet) to Babcock Creek.

The Cariboo River

The Cariboo River south of Unna Lake provides the only alternative egress from the Bowron Lake Chain. It is not a route for novices as there are several rapids and two waterfalls that must be portaged.

The route is impractical and dangerous. In the first 7 kms (4.3 miles) of canoeing Cariboo Falls must be portaged. Then canoes must be taken out and portaged another 7 kms (4.3 miles) around an impassable gorge. This portage is impractical on foot and vehicles from Wells must be arranged.

Paddlers wanting to see parts of the Cariboo River are advised to hike around the falls area. Another paddle route is possible by taking the 3100, or Mathew River, Road west from Barkerville to the Cariboo River. The river meanders from a bridge on the 3100 Road to 15-km- (9.3-mile-) long Cariboo Lake. The egress point, Keithley Creek, is near the south end on the right side of the lake. The logistics of this shuttle are complicated.

The river below Cariboo Lake is difficult and not recommended for canoes.

The headwaters of the Cariboo River, called the Swamp River until relatively recently, are in the ice-fields of the Cariboo Mountains, outside the perimeter of Bowron Lake Provincial Park. The river is a good example of the glacial action that formed this part of the province. It flows through the park from McLeary Lake to Sandy Lake and then turns south to empty into Cariboo Lake in the Quesnel Highlands where all the mountain tops have been ground off by glacial action.

The history of this region is similar to that of the surrounding country where most discovery was a result of the Cariboo gold rush. Early miners pushed up the Cariboo River, then called the Swamp River, searching for new gold streams. But the rich streams were west, draining the Snowshoe Plateau, Antler, Williams and Lightning Creeks.

Cariboo Falls was the site of a proposed power plant as early as 1919. That idea failed, but again in 1938 a crew of men with the Barkerville Development Co. was sent to the falls to do

A cow moose in Babcock Creek, and canoeists approaching the end of Swan Lake, the entrance to Bowron River near right center.

Cariboo Falls on the Cariboo River is a short walk for those camped at Unna or Rum Lakes.

survey work on the Swamp River. The power was to be used for mining around Barkerville. Government funding was to bring a road from Barkerville, but shortly after the survey the idea was dropped.

km 86.4 (mile 53.6) Babcock Creek - 1.2 kms (.75 mile) long
Parks Branch have a patrol cabin a few yards upstream of the mouth of Babcock Creek.

Babcock Creek is named for John Pease Babcock, at one time Deputy Minister of Fisheries. Babcock frequently came here in the autumn with Joe Wendle. He was one of the first to suggest the area become a game sanctuary, no doubt influenced by Wendle's opinion. Both the creek and the lake are still sometimes referred to as Three-Mile Creek and Lake.

"Line canoe" the park brochure says. Sounds easy, right? Fortunately, in most water levels you will be able to paddle several hundred meters (about 1,000 feet) up the creek. Lining is usually done from shore but here the only way is to get wet. Roll up your pant legs, take the bow line and start towing. Your partner can help by pushing and guiding. As the creek becomes shallow the most efficient method will be to shoulder your packs to lighten the load and continue. Parks Branch have built slides to cross the beaver dams which make the route relatively easy compared to the old days. On a sunny day the cold water is welcome, but on a wet, raining or snowing day it is the grunts.

For skiers, the usual winter route is down the east side of the creek, the left when following the recommended route. It is slower than skiing the open lakes, but pleasant, with a good chance of seeing moose, geese, otter and wintering whistling swans.

km 87.6 (mile 54.3) Babcock Lake - 2.8 kms (1.7 miles) long
Paddling into Babcock Lake there is a medium-size sheltered campsite on the left side, #43. It is not ideal as it is shady, summer and winter. Keep to the right side of the lake as the point of land that juts out from the left is surrounded by shallows.

Ahead to the right a long ridge runs the length of Spectacle and Swan Lakes. Called Iltzul, Takulli for forest, it and the Palmer Range to the left form the basin for the lakes. It lies at right angles to the ridges that intersect the center portion of the chain, and to the east of it is the headwaters of the Bowron River. The ridge is part of what is called the Mural Formation.

This Formation is limestone, similar to other formations in the park, but it differs in that there are fossils present, trilobites and primitive corals called archeocyathids.

Babcock Creek flows into the lake near the northwest corner.

Locals formerly knew it as McKenna Creek. McKenna, which now flows into the upper west side of Spectacle Lakes, was earlier called Kokanee Creek for the annual run of landlocked salmon. Pat McKenna was a Barkerville miner who worked on Eight Mile Creek. The mouth of Babcock Creek is reported to be good Dolly Varden fishing.

km 90.4 (mile 56) Skoi Lake Portage - .4 km (.25 mile) long
In the early years of the Game Reserve, Frank Kibbee constructed narrow-gauge railway portages here, later replaced by the Forest Service and Fish and Game Clubs. They were removed years ago in the continuing effort to make the park more of a wilderness experience. The portage is gratefully short.

Along these two portages, or more likely at the end when you have dropped your canoe, there are a few plants to watch for. Baneberry is a leafy plant 1-3 m (3-10 feet) high with erect stems holding two or three leaves broken into divisions of three. The flower is a dense cluster of small white flowers and the fruit a scarlet or white berry. The berries are not edible. Red raspberry blooms here around the end of May, with berries in August. Angelica, squashberry, or high-bush cranberry, false Solomon's seal, and rosy twisted stalk are also common in the area.

km 90.8 Skoi Lake
At one time this was known as Tenas Lake, then Little Lake. Skoi is the Takulli word for little.

In July, at the south end of the lake, water smartweed can be found growing in the calm shallow water and, nearby, purple marsh cinquefoil.

km 91.6 (mile 56.3) Spectacle Lakes Portage - .4 km (.25 mile)
These portages have been in use since the first Indian people entered the lake country, following the salmon upstream, searching for winter food. Carrier Takullis used these same trails and camped at either end, as canoeists do now. Spectacle Lakes' name are a source of conjecture, whether they are named for the beautiful spectacle of scenery, or because from the air the lakes vaguely resemble a pair of spectacles, with Pat's Point being the bridge. Explorer Fred Black called them Sand Lake.

The cabin at the Skoi Lake end of the portage was built by Ernie Holmes, Game Warden on the lakes from 1942 to 1957.

Just past the portage on the east is another small, seldom-visited lake the size of Skoi.

km 92.0 Spectacle Lakes
One kilometer (.6 mile) up the right shore is a small inlet known

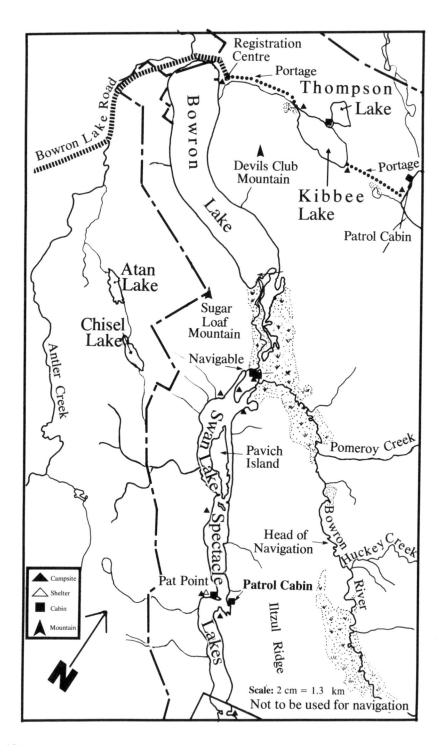

Registration
Centre

Portage

Thompson
Lake

Bowron Lake Road

Bowron Lake

Devils Club
Mountain

Kibbee
Lake

Portage

Patrol Cabin

Atan
Lake

Chisel
Lake

Sugar
Loaf
Mountain

Navigable

Antler Creek

Swan Lake

Pavich
Island

Pomeroy Creek

Spectacle

Head of
Navigation

Bowron River

Huckey Creek

Pat Point

Patrol Cabin

Itzul Ridge

Lakes

Campsite
Shelter
Cabin
Mountain

N

Scale: 2 cm = 1.3 km
Not to be used for navigation

as Deer Bay that makes interesting exploring. There is a large campsite here, #44. One kilometer (.6 mile) further, on the right shore, is another excellent medium-sized campsite.

km 93.6 (mile 58) Spectacle Lakes Campsite #45
This medium campsite is located on the north side of the lake at what is known as the first narrows. Nearby is an old cabin used by Joe Wendle. Stay to the middle of the lake to avoid the shallows that reach out from each shore.

On the right side, south of Pat's Point, there is a group campsite, #46.

km 97.2 (mile 60) Pat's Point and Campsites #47-48
This long neck of land that divides Spectacle Lakes is one of the finest campsites on the chain. There is a group site, a large site and a shelter. The cabin is a former Fish and Game Club cabin. There is also an old trapper's cabin here. Across the lake is the Pat's Point Ranger cabin.

If you listen carefully at night you will hear the call of the great horned owl as it searches for prey. This is a good area to do a little poking around. A short walk north leads to a interesting marsh area. There is also a fair beach here.

This point of land is thought to have been named for Pat McKenna. This spit was owned by Harold Mason and then Vince Halverson and Sid Dannhauer before the area became a park (see People of the Lake).

km 99 Swan Lake Campsite #49
On the left, or west, shore is a medium-sized campsite.

km 100.4 (mile 61) Swan Lake - 5 km (3 miles) long
The Swan Lake narrows is a good place to watch for waterfowl. On the small island south of Pavich Island there is an osprey nest. The large brown and white hawks will often be seen hovering above the lake, waiting to plummet down on a fish.

Swan Lake, once called Angel's Lake, is an extension of the Spectacle Lakes. Canoeists can paddle either side of Pavich Island.

km 101.6 (mile 63) Pavich Island
This island has been known by several names. Originally it was called Deadman's Island. The story was that many Takullis died here from smallpox, a disease they believed came in retribution for their murder of a miner. Although no graves have been found, natives did inhabit the island. It was later named Maternity Island for the cow moose that came here to calf.

The Bowron River and the north end of Bowron Lake, end of the circuit.

Recently, it has been named Pavich Island after Paul Pavich, 1919-1977. The Pavich family moved to the Barkerville area in 1934 where Paul's father was a fur buyer and later ran the Wells cab company. Paul left to serve in the Second World War but returned in 1953. In 1960 he bought Joe Wendle's property on the Bowron River, but it was expropriated for the park. He then built on Bowron Lake and, until his death in 1977, enjoyed the hunting and fishing that the area offered.

km 104.4 (mile 64.8) Campsites
Approaching the end of Swan Lake, you will notice a mound between two bays — the Bowler Hat. There is a medium-sized campsite on the left side of the hat.

The opening on the right is Birch Bay with a large campsite, #50. The narrows to the left leads to the Bowron River. Another campsite is on the extreme left, #52, a medium-sized site. It is a good dry site with fresh creek water. Campsite #51 is a medium-sized site across from #52.

Moose are often seen and heard bellowing in this area on late summer evenings. The prominent mound on the left which has been visible for several kilometers is called the Sugar Loaf.

Winter travellers should stay on the south side of the river, inlet and lakes, and watch for soft ice and open water near the north end of Swan Lake.

A clearing on the left shore marks the site of a 1930s homestead attempt by a couple named Martin.

km 105.6 (mile 65.6) Swan Lake Outlet and Campsites - 0.4 km (.25 mile) downstream
A short stream links Swan Lake with the Bowron River. On a high dry bank to the right is the River Cabin, built by Joe Wendle and used by many canoeists in the years since. Fred Becker also had a cabin on this point of land. Parks Branch also have a patrol cabin nearby on land that was once owned by Paul Pavich.

The campsites on the edge of the Bowron Marsh are the last on the circuit. There is a group site and a medium-sized site, numbers #53-54. If you plan to camp here, arrive early as many canoeists use this as their last night's stop in preparation for canoeing Bowron Lake in the early morning calm.

km 104.8 (mile 65) Bowron River — 4 kms (2.4 miles) long
The Bowron River is fed by two major tributaries — Pomeroy Creek and Huckey Creek. Pomeroy was once called Salmon Creek, an indication of the salmon which spawn here and attract grizzlies each fall, but it is now named for another old-timer, John Pomeroy. He came to Williams Creek in the 1860s, ranched

around Williams Lake, and then returned to the goldfields. He died in 1913.

Huckey was Isabella Hodgkinson, wife of Barkerville's milkman, William Hodgkinson. Bella washed clothes for the Williams Creek miners, and boasted that she was the earliest riser on the creek. Billy agreed and, as her washtubs rattled, he would plead, "Sleep, Bella, sleep." When Bella died in 1911 and was laid to rest in the Camerontown Cemetery, William made a final plea and had the words, "Sleep, Bella, Sleep," carved on her headboard.

The river makes a pleasant upstream paddle for those who want to linger at the campsite for a day or two. It is easily paddled for several kilometres, or miles. It leads into grizzly country. As grizzlies frequent the willow-shrouded banks of the meandering stream during the salmon-spawning season, the river is closed after August 1 to protect the bears' habitat — and canoeists.

Birders would do well to camp here for several days and dig out their field guides, binoculars and spotting scopes. There is an immense variety of birdlife in the Bowron River Estuary, much of it unfortunately unrecorded due to the lack of naturalist staff in recent years.

Spelunkers will be interested to know that on the headwaters of Huckey Creek there is a limestone cave. While it is a large cave, it is reported to have "no redeeming features." Access is difficult and in known bear country, so cavers must check with Parks Branch for directions and permission.

The Bowron River is navigable — with a negligible current — as it flows into Bowron Lake. Paddle slowly and you will see a great assortment of waterfowl, more if you take a side trip into the swamp. You are likely to see coots, mergansers, mallards, widgeon, Canada geese, scaups and more. Since the channel is confusing as you near the river mouth, pay close attention to avoid being lost in the maze of the swamp.

km 108.8 (mile 68.8) Bowron Lake — 7.2 kms (4.5 miles) long

Bowron Lake is the last lake of the circuit, and often seems the longest.

The shortest route is to head for the point of land on the right shore and then follow the shore to the takeout. On the lake's west side are many cottages, the only remaining private property on the lake circuit. They have no road access.

As there is often a wind on the lake, it is a good idea to plan to travel in the morning hours when there is a better chance of winds being in your favor. There are a couple of small beaches on the right side where, if the weather is good, you can spend a last few hours resting from your days of paddling.

You may encounter power boats once you leave the Bowron River. (Bowron Lake is the only lake where power boats are allowed.) The winter substitute is the snowmobile, also restricted to this one lake.

Winter travellers should be careful of frequent open water at the south end of the lake. Warm water flowing out of the river often inhibits ice formation and what appears to be a frozen lake is sometimes only snow-covered water. Cross to the west side of the lake well before reaching the end. Watch for moose crossing the hard-packed snow of the lake and marsh and for the toboggan-like tracks of river otter crossing to and from open water.

km 116.0 (mile 72) End of Circuit
The government wharf for takeout is on the right side of Bowron Lake near the far end. You will have to carry your canoe up a short hill to the parking lot in the campground. Be sure to check out at the visitor centre and deposit your trash bag at the designated place in the campground. Report any bears or unusual sightings of birds or mammals to the registration centre.

There are showers, camping and restaurants at both lodges on Bowron Lake, and accommodation and restaurants in Wells. If you have a day or more left, consider hiking in the area or a visit to Barkerville.

Chapter Eight

Other Canoe Routes

The Bowron River
When the first Cariboo prospectors pushed on from Antler and Williams Creek, the stream they called Bear River became a route leading deeper into the north. Its waters led men toward the Fraser, and from the Fraser into the Omineca country for yet another gold strike. This is not to say it was a well travelled or popular route. It was, and still is, a difficult river with many log jams and several portages.

On its course from Bowron Lake to the Fraser River, the Bowron skirts along the west side of the Cariboo Mountains, crossing the Fraser Plateau. The drainage basin lies in the Columbia Forest region, or what is part of the Sub-Alpine Forest biotic zone. Spruce dominates the vegetation and precipitation is higher than in most of the Interior Plateau. Rain means moisture, and moisture means mosquitoes, so be prepared. Along the river, alder and willow grow on the banks and sandbars and a few cottonwoods and birch are seen.

Wildlife along the river includes moose, black and grizzly bear, marten, fisher, mule deer, caribou, eagles and a variety of waterfowl. At stream mouths there is good angling for rainbow and Dolly Varden trout, and in August salmon spawn in the headwaters.

Part of this canoe route is through the Bowron clear-cut, described as being the largest clear-cut in the world, a man-made feature visible from space. While sections have been replanted and second growth is beginning, the miles and miles of clear-cut have significantly depreciated the canoeing experience.

Route Description
The Bowron is not a river for novices. Log jams and rapids make it tricky and sometimes dangerous. Low water will make it troublesome to maneuver through rock gardens and highwater will make the canyons difficult. Consequently, it is best canoed with a guide.

In the first 16 kms (9.9 miles) of river there are at least six log jams. They completely block the river and while some may be easily passed, at least three require a portage. A little upstream of Eighteen Mile Creek a stretch of rough water begins, but it can be easily run.

Thirty-eight kms (25.5 miles) below the lake a 13-km (8-mile) rapid begins. The first section is boulder-strewn and will require good maneuvering to avoid the rocks. At 45 kms (27.9 miles) a canyon begins which continues until 64 kms (39.7 miles). The water here is grade 3+ and must be scouted before running. The right side is usually the best. Be careful of whirlpools, eddies and rocks on the left side. There is no portage around this canyon. Be prepared to scout the next section. At 64 kms (39.7 miles) Haggen Creek flows in on the right. An old bridge here has caused a log jam around the pilings. Check for a left passage. A road on the east side connects with Highway 16, 60 kms (37.2 miles) north.

Haggen Creek is clear and cold, draining lakes in the Cariboo Mountains. Its stream adds volume to the Bowron and the river picks up speed. Two small rapids are quickly passed and then below Spruce Creek another. Three kms (1.7 miles) downstream from this last rapid there is a long log jam. Check left for a passage. From here the river passes through a large burn and high gravel banks become more frequent. At 101 kms (62.7 miles) there is an abandoned coal mine on the left bank. Canoeists not wishing to run the next section can take out on the right bank where there is road access.

Taspai Creek enters on the left and 1.6 kms (1 mile) downstream the first of three long rapids begins. They are rated grade 3 and require expert skill to navigate. From the third rapid the Highway 16 bridge can be seen. The suggested trip termination is on the left bank below the bridge.

The river below the bridge is more difficult than the upper river and is suitable only for experts. Open canoes will ship water. Five named canyons must be run: Bear, Basket, Portage, Boat and Box. There is 23 kms (14.2 miles) of rapids with 16 individual drops or ledges. At least two portages will be necessary. It is not a recommended route.

Of the first 16 sections the first two begin just below the bridge in Bear Canyon. Left is best. The third canyon is short with high black walls and a left turn; again left is best. The fourth is navigable by a variety of routes and below is 3 kms (1.9 miles) of fast smooth water. The fifth and sixth are short and close together. A portage may be necessary. The right is likely best. At the seventh rough section the river is split by an island and the right will be best.

The next three sections of the 16 drops contain chutes. Either side may be run. One km (1.6 miles) further is a rapid that must be portaged 60 m (200 feet) on the left shore. Scout the next rapid where the river widens. Another portage may be necessary. Three kms (1.9 miles) of fast water leads to the last four rough sections.

A boulder field is first. Try the right. Then there is a small ledge where a chute on the extreme right allows passage. The third must be portaged 30 m (100 feet) on the right. A short canyon follows with high walls and turbulent water. One half a km (0.3 mile) below this canyon is the last rapid. Run it on the left to the right of a large rock.

Cottonwood Island is passed and 0.5 km (0.3 mile) downstream Box Canyon is run, with powerful eddies and boils. From here to the Fraser is 48 kms (30 miles). The river for the most part now meanders and slows considerably. A logging road crosses below Box Canyon. Five km (3 miles) downstream is a dangerous log jam. Start watching for it. Be careful — log jams do not give second chances. Check this obstruction thoroughly before attempting a run.

Beyond the log jam the river meanders to the Fraser River. Three kms (1.9 miles) downstream on the Fraser the Canadian National Railway bridge crosses from McGregor, now a ghost town, to Hansard. Vehicular traffic now uses this bridge as well as the railway so it is a good place to pull out. The road on the left bank leads to Giscome and Prince George.

In summary, the Bowron River is a wilderness stream. It is infrequently travelled so help should not be expected from other parties. As with any river, it is subject to seasonal water level fluctuation and yearly change. The log jams mentioned may wash out, and somewhere else a fallen tree may have begun a new obstacle. Remember that this route description is a guide, not a bible. Travel with caution and always scout ahead.

Summary of Route
Grade - 3
Length - 174 kms (108 miles), 2 to 6 portages
Width - 15 to 30 m (49 to 98 feet).
Vertical Drop - 287 m (941 feet).
Flow - Mean cubic feet per second. At outlet: June 927;
    September 300. At Hansard: June 7,400; September 2,210.
Time to allow - 3 to 5 days
Nearest emergency communication - Bowron Lake lodges
    and Parks Branch at launch; Wells, 27 kms (16.8 miles)
    from launch; Highway 16 near terminus; McGregor,
    across Fraser River.
Accommodation - Bowron Lake Provincial Park camp-
    grounds and lodges, Wells, Prince George.
Maps - National Topographic Series 1:250,000: 93H McBride,
    93G Prince George, 93J McLeod Lake, 93I Monkman Pass.

Chapter Nine
Area Attractions and Services

Bowron Area Trails and Walks

The reconstructed town of Barkerville described further on is only one of the features of this region. Those visitors who wish to stay longer or explore more of the gold-rush era will find the creeks and hills easily reached by a number of roads and trails, several of which have been in use since the early days of the 1860s gold rush. The trails lead to old mine workings, gold camps and towns, hydraulicked areas, mountain lakes and ridges where the whole plateau stretches before you. Park security officers will record your plan and keep a watch for your return. If you check out with them be sure and check back in.

The most accessible historic hike for visitors is the Mt. Agnes-Groundhog Lake Trail. The whole trail will take the better part of a day, but Summit Rock can be reached and a return made in an easy couple of hours walk during the morning or afternoon. The route follows the final few miles of the Cariboo Road, a road walked by many from 1862 to 1885. It leads through Richfield and up Mink Gulch to the summit meadows. Along the way you might see deer, moose, porcupine, red squirrels and grouse. Summit Rock and the meadows was a popular picnic area in Barkerville's heyday. The trail is historic and allows the visitor to capture a little of the feeling of the old days.

The Mount Murray Trail is not so historic, but draws Barkerville visitors because it is the mountain seen at the north end of the street with the beacon-like radio repeater station on top. This route requires more of a climb, but the energetic can still do it in a half-day. Most hikers will prefer to take a day and explore the alpine meadows at the top rather than rush up and down. The panoramic view from the top extends from the Bowron Lakes chain south to Mount Proserpine and takes in all the gold country surrounding Williams Creek. The view alone is worth the climb.

Those looking for a more leisurely walk might try the old road up Stouts Gulch. It was Ned Stout's strike here in 1862 that prompted men like Billy Barker and John "Cariboo" Cameron to try further downstream. The present road was built in 1879 to connect the small summit community of Carnarvon with Williams Creek businesses. The road climbs gradually to the old Canusa mine buildings, from a later era, and the beginning of the Lowhee pit.

Gold was found on Lowhee Creek in 1861 by Richard Willoughby who named it after "The Great Lowhee," a secret miners' protective society on the Lower Fraser River. Much of the gold retrieved from the Lowhee was by hydraulicking, the immense 6.5-km-long (4-mile-long) pit and the extensive tailings at Wells being the result. Although the pit can be hiked, it is rough going and is better travelled by skis in winter. Other trails in the area include the Forest Rose Nature Trail located at the Forest Rose campground north of the airfield. Just 1 km (0.6 mile) long, it is a pleasant afternoon stroll. The town of Wells is an interesting walk, with stops at the museum, community center, churches, Nob, or Snob Hill, and the Jack of Clubs Hotel.

There are many other historical trails in the hills above Williams Creek, but unfortunately most are overgrown to such an extent that they are very difficult to find. With a modern topographic sheet, pre-1900 maps and aerial photos some can be located, but they are suitable only for experienced navigators and hikers. For more information on these trails contact the parks curatorial staff.

Mt. Agnes - Groundhog Lake Trail

Trailhead: Barkerville
Route: Follow Cariboo Road past Richfield, taking the middle Fork at the Courthouse, up to Summit Rock. From there follow ditch line on south side of meadow or road up Jack of Clubs Lake to Groundhog Lake.
Return distance: 12 kms (7.5 miles)
Elevation gain: 490 m (1,607 feet)
Time to Allow: 5 hours
Map: Rough trail map from parks branch or N.T.S. Wells, 93 H/4
Aerial photo: BC5393 No. 057

Bald Mountain - Proserpine Trail

Experienced hikers wishing to extend their tour can continue from Groundhog Lake, where there was once a roadhouse, to Bald Mountain. The trail is indistinct. Travel to the east of Agnes and the lake and continue until you pick up a well-worn trail as it traverses above a small tarn across a rock slide on the east slope. From there a trail can be seen across the valley on Bald Mountain. From Bald Mountain a trail is flagged across Proserpine Mountain to the Conklin Gulch road. This trail is only suitable for experienced hikers and navigators. Check with Parks Branch for further information.
Distance: 81-km (50-mile) round trip from Barkerville

Mt. Agnes, one of the many interesting hikes through the
1860s gold-rush country surrounding Barkerville.

Elevation gain: 500 m (1,640 feet)
Time to Allow: 2-3 days
Map: As for Mount Agnes-Groundhog Lake.

Yellowhawk Creek - Mount Murray Trail
Trailhead: km 5 (mile 3.1) on Bowron Lake Road. Gravel pit on
right. Trail begins on pit's left, or north, side.
Route: Up Yellowhawk Creek. Take left fork at about one hour. At
cabin cut across meadows to Mount Murray's slopes and climb
past two false summits and an alpine tarn to Mount Murray.
Return Distance: 7 kms (4.3 miles)
Elevation gain: 680 m (2,230 feet)
Time to allow: 4 hours
Map: N.T.S. Spectacle Lakes 93 H/3

Stout's Gulch Trail
Trailhead: Begin in Barkerville. Take Richfield Road for 0.5 km

(0.3 mile), then turn right, or west, up Stout's Gulch.
Route: Up Stout's Gulch to summit and return, or continue down Lowhee Creek and the Lowhee Pit to Well's Ski Hill.
Return Distance: 6 kms (3.7 miles) to summit and return. 10 kms (6.2 miles) to Wells.
Elevation gain: 150 m (492 feet)
Time to allow: 2-3 hours to summit, 4 hours to Wells.
Map: N.T.S. Wells, 93 H/4
Aerial photo: BC5393 No.057 or Barkerville Mosaic PM334

Cariboo Road Trail
Trailhead: Begin in Barkerville or Stanley.
Route: From Barkerville proceed to Summit Rock as in Groundhog Lake Trail. Follow indistinct trail along Jack of Clubs Creek to Ella Lake, then down north side of Lightning Creek. Trail is in poor condition, overgrown and washed out in some sections. Check with Parks Branch for more route information before attempting. From Stanley, follow in reverse.
Distance: One-way, 20 kms (12.4 miles)
Time to allow: 2 days
Map: N.T.S. Wells, 93 H/4
Aerial photo: BC5393 No.059 and No.058

Racetrack Flat Trail
Trailhead: End of Antler Creek road.
Route: Drive up Antler Creek from 3100 Road. At about 10 kms (6.2 miles) the road crosses Antler Creek at Sawmill Creek. Just before the ford a road goes to the right. Follow this road. Most cars will have to pull off the road at approximately 1 km (0.6 mile). Follow the road upstream for one hour of walking to the end where there is a small cabin. Cross Antler Creek. Climb hill behind cabin to ditch line, follow ditch line to right for 40 minutes. The trail ends on a large flat which was used in the early 1800s as a horse-racing track. Remains of a roadhouse run by Tom Maloney is at the east end and nearby are two graves. One is that of Jack Emmory who died on Williams Creek in August 1862.
Elevation gain: 200 m (656 feet) from Antler Creek and Sawmill confluence.
Time to allow: 4 hours
Map: N.T.S. Cariboo Lake 93 A/14

Chapter Ten

Visitor Services

Barkerville

Barkerville Historic Park is open year round from dawn to dusk. However, most services are limited to the summer months of May to September, a policy in historical keeping with the mining season of April to October. Placer gold mining required running water, and the long cold winters, with temperatures dropping to -43°C (-45°F) and snow 6 m (20 feet) deep, forced miners south or indoors for winter. Although there is a desire to extend the tourist season beyond summer, few, if any, stores or food services will be open in winter. Parks offices at Barkerville, however, are open all year. There are no accommodations in the park other than campgrounds which have a nightly fee in all campsites and a maximum stay of 14 days.

Campgrounds

Lowhee Campground, on the Wells-Barkerville road east of Wells. Ninety sites, sani-station, pit toilets, fire pits.

Forest Rose Campground, on Bowron Lake Road at km 0.5 (mile 0.3), east of Wells. Forty-eight sites, pit toilets, fire pits.

Government Hill Campground on Reduction Road, above the Cemetery. Twenty-five small sites, not suitable for trailers. Short walk to townsite. Pit toilets and fire pits.

Picnic Grounds

There is a large picnic ground near the entrance to Barkerville town at the north end of the parking lot.

Wells Visitor Services

The 1930s mining town of Wells provides most of the visitor services for the Bowron Lake and Williams Creek area. There is a hotel, two motels and a primitive log cabin court where visitors can experience a miner's cramped, dark life. Further accommodation is offered at Bowron Lake lodges. Groceries and gas are available in town and there are several restaurants with a variety of fare, including one fine restaurant in a restored Barkerville building.

There is a Hard Rock Mining Museum and several local celebrations of interest to visitors. Gold Rush Days and the

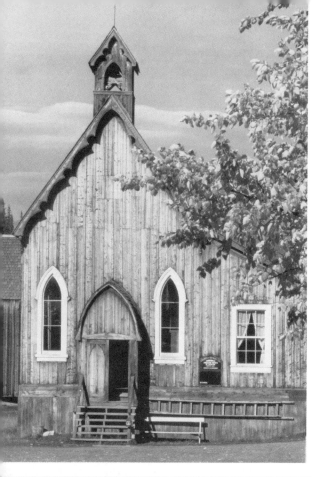

The gold-rush community of Barkerville attracts tens of thousands of visitors every year. St. Saviour's Church, built in 1869 and still in use, is among the original buildings.

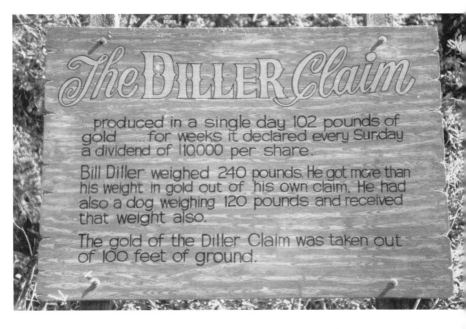

The DILLER Claim

...produced in a single day 102 pounds of gold ....for weeks it declared every Sunday a dividend of 110,000 per share.

Bill Diller weighed 240 pounds. He got more than his weight in gold out of his own claim. He had also a dog weighing 120 pounds and received that weight also.

The gold of the Diller Claim was taken out of 100 feet of ground.

The Diller claim marker at Barkerville shows the riches of Williams Creek. Many claims yielded over $1,000 a foot, with gold at $16 an ounce.

The Joe Wendle and William Bowron houses are among over 40 original buildings in Barkerville. Many others have been restored as part of an ongoing program to restore the gold-rush community.

Island Mountain School of Arts are held in August; there is a Halloween Dance; a Snowball Tournament in February and a curling Bonspiel in March. During summer months the Historical Society offers weekend movies in the old theatre, a fund raising event popular with local residents.

The nearest other supplies and accommodations are at Quesnel on Highway 97. Quesnel is also serviced by daily jet aircraft, B.C. Railway, and bus lines. Wells is serviced by Barkerville Stage Lines.

Bowron Lake Circuit Reservations and Information
D.J. Park Contractors
358 Vaughan Street
Quesnel, B.C. V2J 2T2
(604) 992-3111 Fax (604) 992-6624

Bowron Lake Accommodation, Rentals and Supplies
Becker's Canoe Outfitters Restaurant and Lodge
Box 129, Wells, B.C. V0K 2R0
Quesnel Radio Operator, N698552

Bowron Lake Lodge and Resorts Ltd.
740 Vaughan Street
Quesnel, B.C. V2J 2T5
(604) 992-2733 or Quesnel Radio Operator, N697937

Bear River Merchantile
P.O. Box 251
Wells, B.C. V0K 2R0
Prince George Radio Operator (604) H496699 on Wells Y.P.

Area Accommodation
Jack of Clubs Hotel & Restaurant
Box 109, Wells, B.C. V0K 2R0
(604) 994-3210

Hubs Motel
Box 116, Wells, B.C. V0K 2R0
(604) 994-3313 Fax 994-3237

Wells Hotel and Gallery
Pooley Street
Wells, B.C. V0K 2R0
(604) 994-3427 Fax 994-3494

Whitecap Motor Inn and Campground
Ski Hill Road
Wells, B.C.
(604) 994-3489 Fax 994-3426

Services
Airstrip: east of Wells. Length, 762 m (2,500 feet); elevation, 1,280 m (4,200 feet); paved.

R.C.M. Police: local detachment in Wells. (604) 994-3314

Boat Launching Site: Launching on Jack of Clubs and Bowron Lakes.

Camping and Sani-Station: see Barkerville Provincial Historic Park. Private campgrounds with showers and additional government campsites are located in Wells and at Bowron Lake, 28 kms (17.3 miles) northeast.

Area Information Services
Manager,
Barkerville Historic Townsite
Barkerville, B.C. V0K 1B0
(604) 994-3332

Ministry of Forests
Regional Office
Williams Lake, B.C.
(604) 398-7121

Ministry of Forests
District Office
Quesnel, B.C.
(604) 992-2147

Fish and Wildlife Branch
540 Borland Street
Box 9000
Williams Lake, B.C.
V2G 1R8
(604) 392-6261

Parks Branch
540 Borland Street
Williams Lake, B.C. V2G 1R8
(604) 398-4414

Cariboo Tourist Association
Box 4900
Williams Lake, B.C. V2G 2V8
(604) 392-2226

Cariboo Mountains Wilderness Coalition
P.O. Box 34293, Stn. D.
Vancouver, B.C. V6J 4N8

Chapter Eleven

Birds and Mammals of Bowron Lake Provincial Park

THE BIRDS

This checklist is based on a list compiled by park naturalists in 1973, with additional recent sightings by the author and lake residents. It is not complete and it would be appreciated if further sightings could be sent to the author care of the address on page 124.

Fall sightings are indicated with a "F"; winter sightings, with "W"; uncommon birds are indicated by "U" and known nesting species by "N".

☐ Bittern, American
☐ Blackbird, Brewer's
☐ Blackbird, red-winged
☐ Blackbird, rusty
☐ Blackbird, yellow-headed (U)
☐ Bluebird, mountain
☐ Bufflehead (W)
☐ Buntings, snow

☐ Catbird (U)
☐ Chickadee, black-capped (W)
☐ Chickadee, boreal
☐ Chickadee, chestnut-backed (U)
☐ Coot, American (U)
☐ Cowbird, brown-headed
☐ Crossbill, white-winged
☐ Crow

☐ Dipper - water ouzel
☐ Dowitcher, long-billed (U)

☐ Eagle, bald (N)
☐ Falcon, peregrine (U)
☐ Finch, evening
☐ Finch, gray-crowned rosy
☐ Flicker, northern
☐ Flicker, yellow-shafted
☐ Flycatcher, olive-sided

☐ Goose, Canada (W)
☐ Goose, snow
☐ Goldeneye, Barrow's
☐ Goldeneye, common
☐ Goshawk
☐ Grebe, western
☐ Grebe, red-necked
☐ Grosbeak, evening
☐ Grosbeak, pine
☐ Grouse, blue
☐ Grouse, ruffed
☐ Grouse, spruce
☐ Gull, Bonaparte's
☐ Gull, mew
☐ Gull, ring-billed
☐ Gyrfalcon

☐ Harlequin
☐ Hawk, Cooper's
☐ Hawk, marsh
☐ Hawk, pigeon
☐ Hawk, red-tailed
☐ Hawk, sharp-shinned
☐ Hawk, Swainson's (U)
☐ Heron, great blue
☐ Hummingbird, Anna's
☐ Hummingbird, rufous

- ☐ Jay, gray
- ☐ Jay, Steller's
- ☐ Junco, Oregon (W)

- ☐ Kestrel, American
- ☐ Killdeer
- ☐ Kingbird, eastern
- ☐ Kingfisher, belted
- ☐ Kinglet, golden-crowned
- ☐ Kinglet, ruby-crowned

- ☐ Longspur, chestnut-collared
- ☐ Longspur, Lapland
- ☐ Loon, Arctic (F)
- ☐ Loon, common

- ☐ Magpie, black-billed (U)
- ☐ Mallard
- ☐ Merganser, common
- ☐ Merganser, red-breasted
- ☐ Nighthawk, common
- ☐ Nutcracker, Clark's
- ☐ Nuthatch, red-breasted

- ☐ Oldsquaw (U)
- ☐ Osprey
- ☐ Owl, barred
- ☐ Owl, boreal
- ☐ Owl, great gray
- ☐ Owl, great-horned (W)
- ☐ Owl, pygmy
- ☐ Owl, snowy

- ☐ Pelican, white (F)
- ☐ Pewee, western wood
- ☐ Phalarope, western
- ☐ Pintail
- ☐ Pipit, Water
- ☐ Ptarmigan, white-tailed

- ☐ Raven (W)
- ☐ Red Poll
- ☐ Redstart, American
- ☐ Robin (N)
- ☐ Ruddy duck (U)

- ☐ Sandpiper, Baird's (F)
- ☐ Sandpiper, spotted
- ☐ Sapsucker, yellow-bellied (W)
- ☐ Scaup

- ☐ Scoter, surf
- ☐ Scoter, white-winged
- ☐ Shoveler (U)
- ☐ Shrike, northern
- ☐ Siskin, pine
- ☐ Snipe, common
- ☐ Snipe, Wilson's
- ☐ Solitaire, Townsend's
- ☐ Sparrow, chipping
- ☐ Sparrow, golden -crowned
- ☐ Sparrow, Lincoln's
- ☐ Sparrow, savannah
- ☐ Starling
- ☐ Swallow, barn
- ☐ Swallow, cliff
- ☐ Swallow, rough-winged
- ☐ Swallow, tree
- ☐ Swan, trumpeter
- ☐ Swan, whistling (W)
- ☐ Swift, Vaux's

- ☐ Tanager, western
- ☐ Teal, cinnamon (U)
- ☐ Teal, green-winged (U)
- ☐ Tern, common
- ☐ Thrush, hermit
- ☐ Thrush, Swainson's
- ☐ Thrush, varied

- ☐ Vireo, red-eyed
- ☐ Vireo, solitary
- ☐ Vireo, warbling

- ☐ Warbler, Audubon's (yellow-rumped)
- ☐ Warbler, blackpoll
- ☐ Warbler, MacGillivray's
- ☐ Warbler, magnolia
- ☐ Warbler, orange -crowned
- ☐ Warbler, Tennessee
- ☐ Warbler, Townsend's
- ☐ Warbler, Wilson's
- ☐ Warbler, yellow
- ☐ Waterthrush, northern
- ☐ Waxwing, Bohemian (U)
- ☐ Waxwing, cedar

- ☐ Widgeon, American
- ☐ Woodpecker, downy
- ☐ Woodpecker, black-backed three-toed (U)
- ☐ Woodpecker, pileated (U)
- ☐ Woodpecker, hairy
- ☐ Woodpecker, ladder-backed
- ☐ Woodpecker, northern three-toed
- ☐ Woodpecker, red-headed
- ☐ Wren, winter
- ☐ Yellowlegs, greater (U)
- ☐ Yellowlegs, lesser
- ☐ Yellowthroat

THE MAMMALS

This list includes only the major mammals of the park. There are many more, such as the mice and voles, that have not been recorded. Please send additional sightings to the author at 3487 Auchinachie Road, Duncan B.C. Canada V9L 4A2.

- ☐ Bat
- ☐ Bear, black
- ☐ Bear, grizzly
- ☐ Beaver
- ☐ Caribou
- ☐ Cougar
- ☐ Coyote
- ☐ Deer, mule
- ☐ Fisher
- ☐ Fox
- ☐ Goat, mountain
- ☐ Groundsquirrel, Columbia
- ☐ Hare, varying
- ☐ Lynx
- ☐ Marten
- ☐ Mink
- ☐ Moose
- ☐ Muskrat
- ☐ Otter
- ☐ Porcupine
- ☐ Red squirrel
- ☐ Skunk
- ☐ Weasel, least
- ☐ Weasel, long-tailed
- ☐ Weasel, short-tailed
- ☐ Wolf
- ☐ Wolverine

The martin is inquisitive and agile, able to catch squirrels which are an important part of its food.

Appendix Two

Selected Bibliography

Cochran, Lutie Ulrich. *The Wilderness Told Me*. Quesnel, B.C.: Aveline Moffat Hill, 1964.

Harris, W. Howard. *Ten Golden Years: Barkerville-Wells, 1932 - 1942*. Quesnel, B.C.: Little Shepherd Publications, 1984.

Hong, W.M. *...And So...That's How It Happened*. Quesnel, B.C.: W. M. Hong, 1978.

Ludditt, Fred W. *Campfire Sketches of the Cariboo*. Penticton, Fred W. Ludditt, 1974.

Quesnel Cariboo Observer, Quesnel, B.C.

Skelton, Robin. *They Call it the Cariboo*. Victoria: Sono Nis Press, 1982.

Speare, Jean E. *Bowron Chain of Lakes: Place Names and People*, Quesnel, B.C.: High Plateau Publishing, 1983.

Wright, Richard Thomas. *Barkerville: A Gold Rush Experience*. Duncan: Winter Quarters Press, 1993.

Overlanders. Saskatoon, Saskatchewan: Western Producer Prairie Books, 1985.

Index